Development, Justice and Citizenship

Series Editor
Jean Grugel
Department of Politics
University of York
York, UK

This series responds to the urgent need to explore the multiple challenges of research International Development from the perspective of justice and citizenship Complex issues such as the global inter-connectedness of places, economies, communities, and ideas, the movement of people, the costs of increasingly intensive and extensive models of capitalist growth, the global economy of energy, finance and production, global scarcity, abundance and consumption, security, health and environmental degradation all bring with them human dilemmas that directly affect people in or from the Global South and are at the heart of current agenda for development studies. It seeks to stimulate research for the highest calibre around international development as a question of social, political, economic and cultural justice and global social responsibility. It will showcase theoretical and empirical studies of the multi-level struggles for justice by and ordinary people and the politics and policies that seek to give rise to a fairer and more just global society. The series seeks contributions, therefore, that reveal the multiple ways people operate and engage in forms of struggle for a better world, and that explore the ways states and international actors engage with demands for change. We welcome submissions from scholars across the globe in the form of research monographs, edited collections and shorter, polemic books (pivots) that address this agenda is a direct, scholarly and thought-provoking fashion.

More information about this series at
http://www.palgrave.com/gp/series/14949

Ruth Murambadoro

Transitional Justice in Africa

The Case of Zimbabwe

palgrave
macmillan

Ruth Murambadoro
Johannesburg, South Africa

Development, Justice and Citizenship
ISBN 978-3-030-48091-2 ISBN 978-3-030-48092-9 (eBook)
https://doi.org/10.1007/978-3-030-48092-9

Cover credit: © Melisa Hasan

This Palgrave Macmillan imprint is published by the registered company Springer Nature Switzerland AG
The registered company address is: Gewerbestrasse 11, 6330 Cham, Switzerland

This book is dedicated to my mother Agnes Zvogodii Murambadoro who played a key role in my studies and career development but passed on before this project was completed.

Preface

The entry point of this book is to offer an interpersonal (human-centred) understanding of violence, peace and justice, and the processes that occur to communities in transition to facilitate rebuilding social harmony. Transition in this writing encompasses ongoing transformations in the sociopolitical, economic, cosmological and ecological lives of people in post-colonial Zimbabwe. This shift in focus moves away from a state-centric perspective to the personal and interpersonal levels. The book thus attends to three things: first, it offers a lens to explore the complexities of violence associated with multiparty elections in the period 2000–2008, focusing on lived experiences of people in three rural communities, Buhera, Mudzi and Uzumba. These three areas experienced violence in the period 2000–2008 and were recorded as the major hot spots for the electoral violence of 2008 (*Human Rights Watch* 2008, *Solidarity Peace Trust* 2008).

Second, I focus on effects of state-sanctioned violence at the interpersonal level as a deviation from the mainstream transitional justice discourse which tends to address victims/perpetrators in singular form. I argue that people cannot be reduced to victims or perpetrators because they do not exist in vacuum, rather in relation to others. As such the personal and interpersonal relations (by extension communal) are intertwined and shape both the individual and collective experiences of violence. A focus on the personal and interpersonal effect of violence helps to bring out the interconnectedness of individuals and their surroundings (i.e. one's encounter in relation to their environment). Persons studied in this book locate their being within *imba* (family unit), *musha* (place of origin or homestead) and *mhuri* (the family/clan). Their life exists as a shared enterprise guided by expansive spiritual and moral values that create networks of relations, command behaviours and inform processes of retaining social harmony, whenever it has been compromised.

Third, it engages with the concept of peace and justice concentrating on beliefs, customs and practices embedded in communities that experienced electoral violence in the period 2000–2008. Emphasis is placed on the remedies that local communities enact to address relational harms that occur to the living beings and their extended cosmological or metaphysical community during transitions. I argue that transitional justice as a borrowed Western concept that is being transplanted to African settings, it still needs to be refined to suit local realities. Transitional justice is examined in this book as a value-laden travelling concept that changes as it moves across settings and often creates contested meanings. For instance, while the government of Zimbabwe commissioned in 2018 the National Peace and Reconciliation Commission (NPRC) as an initiative for transitional justice (i.e. providing post-conflict justice, healing and reconciliation), the NPRC Bill (which guides the work of the commission) does not use the term. More so, ordinary people who participated in the public hearings that forged this bill were not using the term. Instead, the concept mostly appeared in the discourse of civil society actors, particularly human rights defenders such as the National Transitional Justice Working Group (NTJWG), who even suggested the South African TRC as a yardstick on which the works of the commission could be determined. I argue therefore that the term transitional justice does not exist in the vocabulary of the local communities covered in this book; instead, various actors at the national and local levels hold varying meanings on justice and the means to acquire it. Accommodating their varying meanings of justice is key to creating initiatives of redress that meet the needs of people.

The term justice in the vernacular languages of participants from Buhera, Mudzi and Uzumba means *kuenzanisa* (creating a balance or making equal), *kunzwana nhunha* (listening to troubling issues), and *kuringanisa* (making amends or creating a balance). It involves *kuraira* (giving counsel), *kuranga* (instilling discipline), *kudzoredzanisa* (reconciling) and *kuripira* (reparations). Justice is conceptualised as a doing word that commands actions, affirmations and interactions to facilitate a process of reflection, engagement and healing to the damaged cosmos. It is constituted through virtues (*Hunhuism*) and the exercise thereof by all members of the social grouping. This understanding of justice brings people together to foster harmony in the cosmological sense. There is no timeframe (multiple temporalities) for the process, because their justice is geared towards retaining a cosmic balance (between the physical and metaphysical) whenever it is disrupted. Transitions and justice covered in this book, therefore, refer to processes of redress that renew the essence of African beings by transforming disruptive encounters and fostering their social harmony in the cosmological sense.

Johannesburg, South Africa Ruth Murambadoro

Acknowledgments

I started working on this book project at a time I was dealing with the untimely passing of my mother. She was a central pillar in my life and losing her had a huge impact on my personal and professional life. Many people have come forth and assisted me to carry on and finish the work. My father Murray though grieving his own loss of a life partner made the time to talk me through my fears and moments of despair. Simbarashe my partner carried the weight in prayer and was a shoulder to lean on. My loving siblings Daniel, Miriam and Walter and in-laws Ressias, Tsitsi and Bridget made time to engage me throughout the research journey. I am grateful for the many colleagues I met while working on my research, most of whom have become family. I give special thanks to Dr. Adam Branch, Professor Lungisile Ntsebeza and Dr. Jimmy Spire Ssentongo for the great engagements we had while I completed a writing fellowship offered by the Centre of African Studies, University of Cambridge. My Ph.D. supervisor's Dr. Cori Wielenga and Professor Alois Mlambo, I thank you for making time to mentor me and the meticulous advice you gave that sharpened my thinking. To my institution the

Wits School of Governance, led by Professor David Everett, thank you for giving me the opportunity to complete my writing away from work.

Various phases of the research that feeds this project were completed with financial support from the Centre of African Studies, University of Cambridge, the Social Science Research Council's Next Generation Social Sciences in Africa Fellowship, with funds provided by Carnegie Corporation of New York SSRC, the University of Pretoria Postgraduate Research Support Grants and the National Institute for the Humanities and Social Sciences-Council for the Development of Social Science Research in Africa (NIHSS-CODESRIA).

I am also grateful for the love and emotional support offered by my friends and relatives, namely, Benjamin Mhishi, Tracey Muradzikwa, Mildred and Terrence Chimbwanda, Liana and Tendai Mutezo, Komborero Mabenge, Wendy Mupaku and Marion Ouma. More so, I am thankful for the many research assistants and participants who gave their time and shared precious encounters that made it possible for me to complete this project. Lastly, to all the people that came through for me, whom I could not mention by name, I appreciate you.

Praise for *Transitional Justice in Africa*

"Grounding her analysis in the understandings and experiences of survivors of state violence in Zimbabwe, Murambadoro exemplifies the intense engagement with local and national histories, with specific languages and conceptual frameworks, and with marginalized communities that is needed if transitional justice is to have meaning. A crucial corrective to the dominant TJ industry and a brilliant contribution to what it might mean to decolonize transitional justice."

—Dr. Adam Branch, *Director, Centre of African Studies, University of Cambridge*

"A timely book on Transitional Justice grounded on experiences of communities on a subject previously under-researched. The book reveals the challenges of rebuilding relationships and transforming communities that have experienced violence from bottom-up using unorthodox yet deeply rooted cultural norms. An important Afro-centric analogy based on the Zimbabwean experience, and a must-read for Transitional

Justice scholars and practitioners to appreciate what communities with deep cultures value most."

—Dr. Webster Zambara *(Ph.D.), Senior Project Leader, Institute for Justice and Reconciliation (IJR), Cape Town*

Contents

Abbreviations

AIPPA	Access to Information and Protection of Privacy Act
AU	African Union
AUTJ	African Union Transitional Justice Framework
CCJP	Catholic Commission for Justice and Peace
CSO	Civil Society Organisation
DANet	DESTINY of Africa Network
DDR	Disarmament, Demobilisation and Reintegration
DRC	Democratic Republic of Congo
ESAP	Economic Structural Adjustment Program
ESC	Electoral Supervisory Commission
HDF	Health Development Fund
ICC	International Criminal Court
ICTR	International Criminal Tribunal for Rwanda
ID	Identity Document
IMF	International Monetary Fund
JOC	Joint Operation Command
MDC	Movement for Democratic Change
MDC-M	Movement for Democratic Change-Mutambara
MDC-T	Movement for Democratic Change-Tsvangirai
MP	Member of Parliament

NPRC	National Peace and Reconciliation Commission
POSA	Public Order and Security Act
SABC	South Africa Broadcasting Cooperation
SADC	Southern Africa Development Community
UMP	Uzumba Maramba Pfungwe
UNISA	University of South Africa
UK	United Kingdom
ZACC	Zimbabwe Anti Corruption Commission
ZAPU	Zimbabwe African People's Union
ZANLA	Zimbabwe African National Liberation Army
ZANU-PF	Zimbabwe African National Union Patriotic Front
ZCTU	Zimbabwe Congress of Trade Union
ZDF	Zimbabwe Defence Forces
ZEC	Zimbabwe Electoral Commission
ZHRC	Zimbabwe Human Rights Commission
ZIMCET	Zimbabwe Civic Education Trust
ZINTE	Zimbabwe Integrated National Teacher Education Course
ZCCU	Zimbabwe Teachers' Association Co-operative Credit Union
ZOU	Zimbabwe Open University
ZUM	Zimbabwe Unity Movement

1

Centring Justice on Human Relations

Abstract In post-independence Zimbabwe, many civilians were subjected to state-sanctioned violence with grave consequences on human relations and harmony at community level. Elitist transitional justice processes employed by the state have not managed to address the relational harms that occur at the interpersonal level, which I argue in this book to be essential for obtaining justice and peace in the cosmological sense. This book offers an interpersonal understanding of violence, peace and justice, by focusing on relational harms that occurred in three rural communities, namely Buhera, Mudzi and Uzumba between 2000 and 2008. This shift from state-centric to the interpersonal level allowed the book to offer a new lens on the efficacy of African justice systems in managing transitions at the community level in post-colonial Africa.

Keywords State-sanctioned violence · Political contestations · Human relations · Relational harm · Transitional justice · Relational justice · State-centric · Social harmony

R. Murambadoro, *Transitional Justice in Africa*,
Development, Justice and Citizenship,
https://doi.org/10.1007/978-3-030-48092-9_1

Introduction

About eight years ago, I started working on transitional justice as a desktop researcher who reviewed secondary literature on conflict and peacebuilding processes in sub-Saharan Africa. Much of the literature I read was fixated on statist justice and the human rights discourse (Boraine 2009; Teitel 2000). The dominant idea that informed this discourse was the assumption that human rights violations emanate from the breakdown of state institutions, which can be fixed by building or rebuilding the collapsed institutions following international laws and standards (Westendorf 2015). This exercise of building or rebuilding the broken institutions involves a range of technocratic processes such as criminal prosecutions, truth commissions, reparations and institutional reform (Lederach 1997). These measures are guided by international laws and standards, particularly, human rights law, humanitarian law and international criminal law.

These legal canons have been universalised and tend to override the needs of survivors of violence because criminal justice is often prioritised as the most politically viable and morally acceptable response to gross human rights violations (Mamdani 2015: 80). For example, the South African Truth and Reconciliation Commission (TRC) set up in 1997 prioritised to criminally prosecute 'serious' human rights violations of the apartheid era, which excluded other human wrongs that did not fit this category even though they engendered long-suffering to the South African population (Mamdani 2015: 81). Mamdani (2009: 2) has criticised the TRC for failing to shift the discourse of justice from the criminal and political to the social. This has been the case in Zimbabwe, with the state-led transitional justice initiatives such as the *Chihambakwe* and *Dumbutshena* Commissions of Inquiry established in 1983 and 1984, respectively, at the height of the Matabeleland massacres, and the current National Peace and Reconciliation Commission which was mandated through the 2013 Constitution, that all failed to give human centred or social approach to the state-sanctioned violence faced by Zimbabweans.

Rendering justice through these elitist mechanisms, Phil Clark (2018) describes in his book *Distant Justice* makes it inaccessible to those who do not understand the Western legal framework they rely on or cannot afford to attend the court hearings. Others are excluded by the sheer fact that the mechanisms are designed to attend to incidents of violence that meet a certain threshold (e.g. prosecuting persons responsible for a genocide or gross violations of international humanitarian law), which leaves non-classified encounters in terms of threshold unaccounted for (McEvoy and McConnachie 2013). Yet a lot of money and time is invested by international donors and state actors rendering these legal mechanisms, which in many ways exceed the resources required by some of the affected parties to exercise justice.

An example can be made of the International Criminal Tribunal for Rwanda (ICTR) set up post the 1994 genocide, which has been criticised for being slow, expensive and detached from the Rwandan community (Clark 2010, Wielenga 2014). Between 1994 and 2007 the ICTR had spent more than one billion US$ on its court proceedings which indicted 90 high-level perpetrators of the genocide, made 72 arrests and completed 33 cases, 18 of which were convicted and five were acquitted (Dieng 2011). The ICTR made strides with regard to advancing the international criminal justice framework and prosecuting some high-level genocide perpetrators but fell short on administering justice to the greater population of Rwanda (Batamuliza 2009).

To date there is, therefore, limited successes in terms of violence-stricken communities obtaining justice through the state or international legal bodies and the human rights discourse. Moreover, transitional justice processes have not made an interest in attending to the relational harms that occur at the interpersonal level, which in many respects require much more than a technocratic proceeding or preserving just the rights of a single subject directly affected by violence. Few writings in Africa have looked into interpersonal experiences of persons in violence-stricken communities with the exception of Holly Porter (2016) '*After Rape: Violence, Justice and Social Harmony in Uganda*', Shannon Morreira (2016) '*Rights after Wrongs: Local Knowledge and Human Rights in Zimbabwe*' and Gabrielle Lynch (2018) '*Performances of Injustice: The Politics of Truth, Justice and Reconciliation in Kenya*'. I am focusing on Zimbabwe looking at understandings of violence, justice and peace that draw on accounts of participants who encountered state-sanctioned violence associated with the political contestations between the Zimbabwe African National Union Patriotic Front (ZANU-PF) and the Movement for Democratic Change (MDC)[1] parties in the period 2000–2008. Working with several communities in Zimbabwe that encountered state-sanctioned violence during this era, I learned that political contestations have infiltrated family/clan structures at the community level and destroyed the human and social relations of people. It has become harder for members of the same family/clan to trust each other or work collectively when they belong to different political groupings resulting to the weakening of the interpersonal ties and values (i.e. social fabric) that hold communities in harmony.

Even though this book is focusing on Zimbabwe, it links with global issues as it deals with contemporary debates on the global peace project and the failure of technocratic state-led transitional justice processes to address past injustices in post-colonial African communities. Transitional justice remains a key component of the global peacebuilding project because of the anticipation to hold to account perpetrators of violence, bring peace and social harmony to violence-stricken communities. In the African region, both the African Union (AU) and the Southern African Development Community (SADC) have been working on policies related to transitional justice to inform the processes that ought to occur on the continent. From the draft policy of the AU, namely the AU Transitional Justice Framework (AUTJ), this regional body emphasises that transitional justice ought to be anchored on African understandings of justice, which raises the growing need to address knowledge gaps in the African context (Wachira 2016: 6). At the global level, both the United Nations (UN) and European Union (EU) have supported the view of establishing transitional justice processes that incorporate justice processes exercised by communities in the Global South (Wachira 2016).

On the one hand, governments, practitioners, scholars and global actors are grappling with developing an Africa-centred conceptual framework for transitional justice. On the other hand, communities affected by state-sanctioned violence in Zimbabwe have been left to rely on their own means of healing and redress, which this book argues are processes of justice that have been silenced in mainstream peacebuilding literature. These people-driven justice processes are 'relational', or 'connective' and they permeate the complex network or web of relations that hold local communities together. This web of relations includes relationships between people (physical human beings) and their extended cosmological or metaphysical community. As such, their social fabric thrives when there is a plausible relationship between people and their cosmological community because the survival of the community depends on the entire community (physical and metaphysical) functioning interdependently.

A contribution of this book is the grounded[2] understandings of violence, justice and peace that draws on accounts of participants from Buhera, Mudzi and Uzumba[3] who encountered state-sanctioned violence associated with the political contestations between the ZANU-PF and MDC parties in the period 2000–2008. I focus on the human experience to establish their understanding of the harms created on their personhood, community and the environment they live in. I immersed myself in these three communities because they were hot beds for violence during the elections held between 2000 and 2008. My familiarity with the local communities as an insider-outsider gives impetus to local processes of justice in that this research brings foregrounded perspectives on transition and justice. I have referred to myself as an outsider-insider because Buhera is my rural home and Mudzi is an area where my father spent several years working for the local council after Zimbabwe gained independence. Owing to the time my father spent in Mudzi, I acquired several relatives who have become important members of my family. My ties to Uzumba emanate from a relative in Buhera familiar with one of the participants (*babamunini* Mugezo who comes from this area but has been forced to flee to Asia after encountering violence in 2008). These people became key players in my study especially by linking me to participants who enabled me to understand the underlying causes of the violence that has occurred, and the processes observed or still required to restore social harmony.

Putting a human being behind encounters of violence provides perspectives that give new meanings to justice. Human beings embody a spirit, body, mind, space, emotions, identity and a lived reality, which most literature on peacebuilding and transitional justice often overlook. Their personal narrative does not only become a story, but rather a lens on which to understand human beings, their experiences and their needs when they have encountered violence. As such, state-sanctioned violence in Zimbabwe cannot be viewed as stand-alone incidents, but cyclical, and initiatives of justice become obscured if they fail to grasp the personal and interpersonal experiences. This entails humanising the lived experiences of survivors of state-sanctioned violence through a purposive critical reflection of their stories and the trajectories they have followed since their encounters.

Justice imagined in this writing begins with the human experience (Pillsbury 2019) and is grounded in people's processes of reinforcing collective values, norms and aspirations to counter violence. The notion of transition covered by the book refers to a state of flux in which justice processes driven by individuals and the collective facilitate the renewal of their essence and addresses all aspects of their life that is disrupted by violence. It is therefore not momentary, but a process that in many respects takes the whole journey of a person's life. The outlook created presents the trajectories of human life in both retrospective, present and futurist terms, and the overlapping encounters that shape their experiences across space and time.

Book Outline

The book covers six chapters. In Chapter 1, *Centring Justice on Human Relations* I unpacked the key themes covered in the book that include relational harms, transitional justice, social fabric, social harmony, interpersonal relations and interpersonal justice within the context of Zimbabwe. Discussions around these themes give the outline of the context in which transitional justice will be conceived throughout the book and in the broader discourse of peacebuilding from a local turn.

Chapter 2, *Violence, Transitions and Relational Harms*, adopts a sociopolitical historical approach to give context to the transitions that have occurred in the lives of participants covered in the study, which coincides with key historic moments in Zimbabwe's colonial and post-colonial trajectory. I deploy local terminology for violence to bring out the nature of harms experienced and the impact on co-values of the studied communities.

In Chapter 3, *Harm, Displacement and Interpersonal Justice* I focus on the life history of *babamunini* Mugezo from Uzumba who was attacked during the post-March 2008 electoral violence and now lives in exile. This chapter provides a vivid account of the complexities of human relations and the continuities and discontinuities of these relations in the presence of harms and pursuit of justice.

In Chapter 4, *Spirituality, Rituals and Remedy* I draw on the cosmological argument to tease out ways in which the studied communities understand their realities and the remedies they seek to address violence. My central thesis is that spiritual justice contributes to repairing human relations and the psychosocial effects of violence in the studied communities through sanctions, rituals, ceremonies and reparations.

Chapter 5 *Discourses on Transitional Justice: A National Dialogue* discusses the deliberations that occurred during the national dialogues on the NPRC bill. I pose that the national deliberations failed to reach a consensus on values that should contribute to establishing a new political order in Zimbabwe and the social and spiritual did not seem to be a priority in the framework that emerged.

The book concludes with Chapter 6 *Transitional Justice in Zimbabwe: Myth or Reality?* This chapter provides a recap of the main debates covered in the book and suggestions on the implications of socio-cultural values of the studied communities to the peacebuilding discourse.

Notes

1. Many research participants treated the Movement for Democratic Change-Tsvangirai (MDC-T) faction as the MDC because Morgan Tsvangirai was the founding leader of the MDC. Hence, even though the MDC split in 2005 (Sachikonye 2011) resulting to two formations of MDC that competed in the 2005 and 2008 elections, i.e. the MDC-T and MDC-Mutambara (MDC-M), whenever participants mentioned MDC they were referring to Tsvangira's faction, the MDC-T.
2. I draw on 37 interviews and four focus group discussions conducted with participants from Buhera, Mudzi and Uzumba districts between 2015 and 2019, as well as the government-led public hearings on the National Peace and Reconciliation Commission (NPRC) Bill that occurred in 2016 and

2017. In April 2016 and March 2017, the Zimbabwean parliament hosted a series of public hearings to solicit the views of the citizens on the draft bill of the National Peace and Reconciliation Commission. This bill was initially gazetted on the 18th of December 2015, amidst pressure from the civil society for the government to provide a policy framework to enable the Peace Commission to be instituted (*National Transitional Justice Working Group* 2016). Parliament organised public hearings to provide the local population with an opportunity to participate in framing the policy document that would guide the activities of the Peace Commission. About 200 to 400 members of the public attended each hearing on the NPRC bill. I and in some instances my research assistants observed public hearings held in Bulawayo, Chinhoyi, Harare, Marondera and Mutare and gained insights that provide this book with deeper knowledge on the perceptions of the broader Zimbabwean community relating to issues of transitional justice. All names of participants covered in the book have been replaced with pseudonyms to retain their anonymity.

3. Mudzi and Uzumba are both in Mashonaland East Province, and Mudzi is a district less than 10 km from the Zimbabwe-Mozambique border along Mozambique's Tete Corridor. Mudzi district is largely rural and the local people are fluent in chiBudya, Tonga and chiToko which fall under the Shona language group (*Zimbabwe National Statistics Agency* 2012). Uzumba is a constituency under Uzumba Maramba Pfungwe district also a rural community within Mashonaland East province. The constituency covers eight wards Mukuru Anopamaedza, Marowe, Nhakiwa, Manyika, Musosonwa, Nyamhara, Chigwarada and Chikwira. The main dialect spoken in Uzumba is chiBudya. Buhera is a district and rural area in Manicaland province. Chinjanja (a sub-dialect of Zezuru), chiZezuru and chiNdau are the main Shona dialects spoken by most people, except for isiNdebele in the Gwebo village. This Ndebele-speaking population emigrated from the Matabeleland region during the colonial area, after they had been dispossessed of their land under the Land Appointment Act of 1930. Many people in all three sites are sheltered in homes made up of brick or mud walls with thatched, zinc or asbestos roofing. As communities in the margins, the people use pit or blare toilets for sanitary purposes, rely on firewood for cooking, candles for lighting and borehole or stream water for drinking and personal hygiene.

References

Batamuliza, E.A. 2009. The Role of the International Criminal Tribunal for Rwanda in Building Sustainable Peace. Masters Dissertation, Royal Roads University, Canada.

Boraine, A. 2009. South Africa's Truth and Reconciliation Commission from a global Perspective. In *Peace Versus Justice? The Dilemma of Transitional Justice in Africa*, ed. C.L. Sriram and S. Pillay, 137–152. Scottsville, South Africa: University of KwaZulu-Natal Press.

Clark, P. 2010. *The Gacaca Courts, Post-Genocide Justice and Reconciliation in Rwanda: Justice Without Lawyers*. New York: Cambridge University Press.

Clark, P. 2018. *Distant Justice: The Impact of the International Criminal Court on African Politics*. Cambridge: Cambridge University Press.

Dieng, A. 2011. Capacity-Building Efforts of the ICTR: A Different Kind of Legacy. *Northwestern University Journal of International Human Rights* 9 (3): 403–422.

Lederach, J.P. 1997. *Building Peace: Sustainable Reconciliation in Divided Societies*. Washington, DC: USIP Press.

Lynch, G. 2018. *Performances of Injustice: The Politics of Truth, Justice and Reconciliation in Kenya*. Cambridge: Cambridge University Press.

Mamdani, M. 2009. Response by Mahmood Mamdani. *International Journal of Transitional Justice* 3 (3): 470–473.

Mamdani, M. 2015. Beyond Nuremberg: The Historical Significance of the Post-Apartheid Transition in South Africa. *Politics & Society* 43 (1): 61–88.

McEvoy, K., and K. McConnachie. 2013. Victims and Transitional Justice: Voice, Agency and Blame. *Social & Legal Studies* 22 (4): 489–513.

National Transitional Justice Working Group 2016. *NPRC Bill Is Unconstitutional.* Available from http://www.ntjwg.org/article.php?id=161. Accessed 14 April 2019.

Pillsbury, S.H. 2019. What Is Relational Justice? Loyola Law School, Los Angeles Legal Studies Research Paper No. 2019-09. Available from https://ssrn.com/abstract=3338052. Accessed 30 November 2019.

Porter, H. 2016. *After Rape: Violence, Justice, and Social Harmony in Uganda*. Cambridge: Cambridge University Press.

Sachikonye, L. 2011. *When a State Turns on Its Citizens: 60 Years of Institutionalised Violence in Zimbabwe*. Oxford: African Books Collective.

Teitel, R.G. 2000. *Transitional Justice*. Oxford: Oxford University Press.

Wachira, G.M. 2016. *The African Union Transitional Justice Policy Framework: Promise and Prospects*. Available from http://www.africancourtresearch.com/wp-content/uploads/2016/07/The-African-Union-Transitional-Justice-Policy-Framework-Wachira-GM.pdf. Accessed 12 September 2019.

Westendorf, J.K. 2015. *Why Peace Processes Fail: Negotiating Insecurity After Civil War*. Boulder: Lynne Rienner Publishers.

Wielenga, C. 2014. Reconciliation from the Top Down? Government Institutions in South Africa, Rwanda and Burundi. *Strategic Review for Southern Africa* 36 (1): 25–46.

Zimbabwe National Statistics Agency 2012. *Census 2012 National Report*. Available from http://www.zimstat.co.zw/sites/default/files/img/National_Report.pdf. Accessed 23 August 2019.

2

Violence, Transitions and Relational Harms

Abstract Research about political violence in Zimbabwe has focused on violent encounters as single momentary episodes yet lives of studied communities exist in a trajectory that cannot be isolated into a monolithic past or future. By revisiting the violent encounters of participants in Buhera, Mudzi and Uzumba, this chapter provides a lens to understand lived experiences of local communities and to generate new perspectives on violence, peace and justice. A focus on the communal effect of violence helps to establish the shared responsibility that individuals have to others in the community, because life in this setting is a shared enterprise. Within this shared enterprise, expansive spiritual and moral values guide their network of relations and processes of retaining social harmony, whenever it has been compromised.

Keywords Transition · Post-colonial · Coloniality · Tolerance · African being · *Hunhu* · *ukama* · Intrusion · Raid · Chaos · Disrupt

R. Murambadoro, *Transitional Justice in Africa*,
Development, Justice and Citizenship,
https://doi.org/10.1007/978-3-030-48092-9_2

Introduction

Several scholars have written about transitions in Zimbabwe drawing on the pre-colonial to post-colonial encounters, for example Alois Mlambo (2014), Ndlovu-Gatsheni (2009), Brian Raftopoulos (2009) and Terrence Ranger (1967, 2004). The work of Nyere (2016) points out that,

> Prior to colonialism, the political landscape in Zimbabwe was vitiated by contestations and fighting between tribes and civilizations that existed in the geography of present-day Zimbabwe. The British explorers and settlers' arrival on Zimbabwean soil was equally marred by harsh, feigned, vicious and aggressive intentions and actions. Political independence in Zimbabwe was consummated by violent means together with guerrilla warfare. Governance in post-colonial Zimbabwe has been, by and large, enforced through violence and the threat of violence. (Nyere 2016: 94)

This suggests that violence is not a new phenomenon to the psyche of Zimbabwe's populace, but what has changed overtime is the political muscle behind it. Largely, the violence covered in this book has been fuelled by state actors and thus politically motivated. In this chapter, I turn to the lived experiences of research participants to provide a context-driven account of the sociopolitical transitions they have witnessed which coincide with key historical moments in Zimbabwe. Though my research focused on the period 2000–2008, narratives of violence shared by some of the research participants dated back to the 1960s, a period when Zimbabwe experienced a protracted war, dubbed Second *Chimurenga*[1] (Mlambo 2014). As such, my discussions in this chapter will move between the colonial and post-colonial era to establish the multi-variant temporalities that shape the perceptions of communities under study on issues of violence, transition, harm, social harmony and interpersonal relations. But first, I discuss life in the colony as a prodigy to the state of coloniality that exists in Zimbabwe creating asymmetric power relations between the state and the citizenry, and the ensuing transitions.

Life in the Colony

The war of liberation or Second *Chimurenga* as experienced by participants in the study started as an insurgency that spread from Zambia into Mashonaland West and Central provinces of Zimbabwe, and from Mozambique to Mashonaland East and Manicaland provinces (Mlambo 2014). The book covers three communities in two of the provinces that were infiltrated by this war, i.e. Mudzi and Uzumba in Mashonaland East province and Buhera in Manicaland. Commenting on the volatility of Uzumba area during the struggle, *babamunini* Mugezo (a 50-year-old man) stated that,

> Our community was very dangerous to live in because the liberation fighters had been crossing into Mozambique and Zambia for training then penetrate Rhodesia through the border communities, like ours. ZANLA fighters had even set up camps in our village and often made appearances in our communities which made the government to enforce strict surveillance in our areas.

The said Zimbabwe African National Liberation Army (ZANLA) forces were the military wing of ZANU-PF, a militant black nationalist movement formed during the colonial period (Kriger 2003). The ZANLA fighters used to hide from Rhodesian forces by assimilating into the communities of African people settled around the borders of Zimbabwe with Zambia and Mozambique. These communities were seemingly easier to infiltrate because of similar cultural identities among African populations (Kriger 1991).

The Rhodesian government reacted to the infusion of guerrilla elements in the rural areas by setting up protected villages in 1975 which the participants labelled *maKEEPS*. The villagers ended up building temporary shelters in the KEEPS which were surrounded by a security perimeter of a high fence. The enclosed villages were manned by armed security personnel, and every entrance had soldiers (Kriger 1991). Villagers needed to sign off a register when they went out of the camp during the day and sign back in the evening. They only came out when going to their fields for cultivating or harvesting because they were located outside the camp. Children at schooling age would also go out to attend school. But, no one could stay outside the camp after dusk unless they had a special permission in which they would have stated their whereabouts. The gates of the camp were locked at about 5:30 pm or sunset and a reconciliation of the register/roll call was done. Anyone who was absent without special permission would be enlisted for interrogation and possibly manhunt. *Babamunini* Mugezo and *vatete* Chama (a 49-year-old woman from Mudzi) lived in KEEPS between 1975 and 1979, and these encounters summarise their livelihood in Mudzi and Uzumba during the Second *Chimurenga*.

Sekuru Dengenya a 72-year-old man who lives in Buhera mentioned that between 1965 and 1979 villagers in his area encountered a lot of violence, especially through contacts with the Rhodesian army or *madzakutsaku* (an ancillary operation in the Rhodesian forces) and *magandanga* (guerrilla fighters), because the populace was expected to be loyal to both parties. Villagers were expected to attend *mapungwe* (night vigils) organised by *magandanga* (ZANLA militants), and *sekuru* Dengenya often went to the vigils in Nyazvidzi (a village within Buhera). The night vigils involved singing, dancing and schooling about the liberation struggle.

At one point in 1978, a neighbour to *sekuru* Dengenya was attacked when other villagers had gone for a vigil in Nyazvidzi. *Magandanga* raided the neighbour's homestead and attacked the man of the house on allegations of being an agent for Rhodesian forces. This neighbour had been working at the District Administrator's office in Buhera and being an employee of the regime that was oppressing the black population was considered betrayal of the struggle to end colonialism. During the attack, ZANLA militants beat *sekuru* Dengenya's neighbour until he died and ordered his wife to get a spear to cut him into pieces. She was also forced to dig a shallow grave in the middle of the field within their compound where his remains were dumped. Other villagers only got to know about the incident several days later, when co-workers of the deceased started asking about his whereabouts which led the police to conduct investigations until the truth surfaced.

There was strong surveillance and policing of people's movement and activities during the armed struggle. Both the Rhodesian army and guerrilla fighters patrolled the villages and unleashed violence from both ends.

Vatete Chama stated that 'Rhodesian forces beat, killed and maimed anyone suspected of collaborating with freedom fighters, and most of these security forces were black people like you and me'. In describing the black security forces, she was referring largely to *madzakutsaku* who were an ancillary entity within the Rhodesian forces specially trained to police people from their own communities. This black on black violence eroded trust among the black population and created hatred. The issues were never addressed when the war ended and could be the bases of some continued family tensions that resurfaced during the post-colonial era.

Research participants shared that the ZANLA forces used to mobilise the youth to gather information on the activities of fellow community members. They would beat and kill anyone suspected of cooperating with the government. Pungwes (vigils) were conducted at night led by freedom fighters and those accused of being sell-outs would be named and dealt with. A sell-out was regarded as someone *ari kudya nemuvengi* (who is dining with the enemy or benefitting from the enemy). Black people who worked for the Rhodesian forces were equated to having a transactional relationship with the 'enemy'. For instance, *vatete* Chama's paternal uncle was murdered in Uzumba by ZANLA forces on allegations of being a sell-out. He had been operating a tuck shop business that was doing well, but the jealous of fellow community members caused others to fabricate a story linking him to Rhodesian forces.

Several participants concurred that the violence they witnessed during Chimurenga (the war) was triggered by enmity within communities. *Babamunini* Mugezo mentioned that 'when people did not see eye to eye, on grounds of jealous or unresolved dispute, they could make a story which implicates you as a sell-out. It became your word against mine'. This kind of interpersonal rifts has continued into the post-colonial period. *Mama* Makina a representative of the civil society who spoke about violence during the public hearings of the NPRC bill in Chinhoyi stated that,

> The problem in Zimbabwe's political landscape is that political leadership in the ruling party is the same leadership that was there before 1980. Many of them where trained to be violent during the war and continue to act violently. This has been planted into the citizenry.

Her views suggest that violence was engrained by experiences of the colonial era, and the country is suffering from remnants of coloniality. Colonialism was the process of conquest which resulted in African states being governed by a settler government of Europeans (Maldonado-Torres 2007; Ndlovu-Gatsheni 2013). Coloniality is the logic of colonialism, established through a network of relations of exploitation, domination and control of the means of production in ways that dehumanise, engender disparities and prejudice some members of the society (Quijano 2007; Mamdani 1996). At the core of coloniality is an imbalance of power that affects all aspects of social existence of beings, including gender, sexuality, interpersonal relations, spirituality, language and race (Quijano 2000).

The British-led Lancaster House Conference in 1979 involving the Patriotic Front, represented by Joshua Nkomo and Robert Mugabe, and the Rhodesian government represented by Ian Smith and Bishop Abel Muzorewa, simply ended tensions between the Rhodesian regime and nationalist movements. The conflicting parties signed the Lancaster House Agreement, a deal that provided for: (i) the holding of open elections allowing all citizens to vote, (ii) a new Constitution upholding universal suffrage, and (iii) a ceasefire between armed groups (Mashingaidze 2010). The *magandangas* that were operating in Buhera, Mudzi and Uzumba were moved to assembly points for the demobilisation programme, for example a DDR camp for Buhera was set up at Dzapasi in Nyashanu village. New elections were held in 1980 and the ZANU-PF party won the majority. It took overpower from the Rhodesian government, a process that is often equated to decolonisation. However, the bonds of coloniality (i.e. logic of oppressing, undermining and eliminating the so-called other) were not dismantled, and this continues to haunt the Zimbabwean populace as discussed in the rest of the chapter.

Post-independence Euphoria

When independence was declared in 1980, the people in Buhera, Mudzi and Uzumba entered a new phase of transition, that was characterised by disarmament of armed groups, electoral democracy and socio-economic development, at least for about two decades. This has rendered some participants to consider the first decade after independence a period of euphoria. *Sekuru* Dengenya explained that 'everyone belonged to ZANU-PF and supported it because it was the in thing'. ZANU-PF was presented as the liberating party.

Independence brought a sense of freedom on the rural populace because *magandanga* and *madzakutsaku* had stopped terrorising their communities. People were now able to live without the fear of being attacked. Participants described their state of freedom by indicating that people were able to move freely, they were rebuilding their homes, getting paying jobs in the city, others went back to school and some *vaizvirimira* (went into farming), all of which brought a sense of progress. This suggests that freedom was the absence of direct violence or threat of violence. For example, around 1980 Uzumba Maramba Pfungwe (UMP), i.e. the whole district, had one secondary school, which was not even formal because during the colonial era there were two types of secondary education. The first route was called F2, and it offered basic vocational skills like carpentry, cookery, building and sewing. From F2, no one would go into Advanced level or tertiary training but blue color work or self-employed. The second route was F1; it offered secondary education that enabled one to go to Advanced level and university study. This route was mostly reserved for the white student and a few black elites. Majority of the black people ended at either primary school or took the F2 route (Edwards and Tisdell 1989; Kanyongo 2005).

At independence, the F2 school in UMP was turned into F1, and more F1 schools were built, such that the whole district ended up with more than 21 secondary schools, which changed the education level of the rural populace including those from Uzumba constituency. The government increased student intake in the whole country between 1980 and 1990, for primary school enrolments improved from 819,586 to 2.274,178 (Kanyongo 2005: 69). Secondary school enrolments also changed significantly from 66,215 to 695,882 in the same period (Kanyongo 2005: 69). Edwards and Tisdell (1989) point out that increased school enrolments after independence were necessitated by government's recruitment of expatriate teachers from Australia, Britain and Canada. It also rolled out hot seating (an arrangement where half of the school population attends either morning or afternoon class sessions) and on-the-spot teacher training under the Zimbabwe Integrated National Teacher Education Course (ZINTE) (Kanyongo 2005).

More people in the communities under study attended school because of the prospects for a better job that comes with being educated. For instance, participants shared that the first cohort of students that completed Ordinary level in Uzumba in 1985 (even with two subjects) managed to secure jobs in the police force, teaching (including as relief teachers) and clerical posts. By the year 2005, Uzumba had at least ten secondary schools offering Advanced level. The literacy level in Zimbabwe had improved to a total of 90.7% (i.e. 94.2% for males and 87.2% for females), even though throughput rates of the rural populace remained low (Kanyongo 2005). Arguably, the increasing literacy level, and migration to the city for employment as well as access to disposable income influenced how the research participants understood the changes that occurred to their sociopolitical and economic environment.

Over a period of two decades, elections were held in 1980, 1985, 1990 and 1995, and the research participants indicated that the rural electorate did not necessarily feel obliged to attend political rallies of the ZANU-PF party. *Babamunini* Mugezo said '*Pakatosvika kaperiod kekuti zvekuenda kurally zvaiitwa nevanhu vakapusa* (it got to a point that attending a political rally was considered an activity of the foolish), because the war is over and there was no reason for political action'. Political coercion often occurred from among neighbours because one would not have reason to remain behind when fellow community members were congregating. There were also political commissars who enticed the congregants to attend meetings by offering food handouts or inviting a prominent figure such as a minister. *Sekuru Dengenya* commented that no villager wanted to miss out on either of those two incentives.

This view could have been fuelled by the existence of an abyssal line (De Sousa Santos 2007) between political elites and the villagers. Most political leaders of the ZANU-PF party, for instance government ministers and parliamentarians, though elected through a constituency seat within their rural home, they resided in the city and managed their constituencies from the city. When they visited their rural homes for political rallies or to hand out donations, they often came in driving expensive vehicles (four-wheel drives) and dressed luxuriously in elegant suits or clothing. Their audience in the village was not affluent (in terms of materialist economic muscle) to match the lavish lifestyle portrayed by politicians at the rallies. This often created the perception that everything good is *chirungu* (literary meaning English but figuratively refers to European modernity); therefore, it comes from the city (an inherited embodiment of European modernity), where these elites were residing. Here, the city was Harare, an urban area that was captured from the African chief Neharawe in 1890 by colonial administrators under the British South Africa Company's Pioneer Column who renamed it Salisbury after Lord Salisbury, the then prime minister of Britain (Norman 2015: 19–22). Salisbury and present-day Harare became the seat of both the colonial and post-colonial government. Any development or progress of one's life in the village would be viewed considering the posture of the elites from the city who occasionally visited their rural homes and brought with them goodies, such as bread, margarine, jam and rice.

While these differences were playing out, they created a false consciousness among state actors and the villagers, centred on inferiority—a caricature of the abyssal line. As such, those people who lived in the city (i.e. politicians and some of their own relatives who had migrated for work) were viewed in high regard to those remaining in the village. In terms of political views, the ruling party was 'the in thing' as suggested by *sekuru* Dengenya because it was considered the brains of the state and held the seat of government. Many of the political figures in the party were educated people; for example, the leader of ZANU-PF Robert Mugabe had several qualifications including a Bachelor of History and English, Bachelor of Education, a Bachelor and Master of Laws among others (Norman 2015). A human rights defender Mr. Brian Kagoro while commenting on Mugabe's legacy made the remark that the former president had an interest in engaging with educated fools than uneducated people (SABC Digital News 2019), which made him invest a lot in education after the country attained independence. In the views of some research participants, these bureaucrats were revered for their intellectual acumen, a stature that rendered the uneducated masses many of whom were in the village incompetent of understanding the political discourse and intricacies of governance.

Babamunini Mugezo explained that many in his community were not bothered to participate in political deliberations because it was a realm of the elite, those living in the city, where there is *chiedza* (literally means light and figuratively being intelligible and developed). Disparities of livelihoods between people living in the city and those in the village were dire, for instance road infrastructure, electricity and telecommunications among others (Tevera 1997). People in the city were seemingly more familiar with current affairs because they could get information from varying media sources. Urban settlers could access information through telegraph, telephone, the television, radio, print media, whereas those *vari kumusha* (in the village) relied on radio, word of mouth or reading newspapers sent by their relatives, which were usually for use as toilet paper in the blair toilet.

Sekuru Dengenya commented that this sense of the villager being incompetent of comprehending political discourse made the ruling party complacent,

> On the side of the ruling party, from independence it was in slumber, they assumed that they would always be in power. Whatever they do people can vote for them. Hence by 2000, it came as a shock that people could rise against them, they were not prepared to lose power. The only weapon they had was -violence- they had used it previously in war and to exterminate the alleged dissidents in Matabeleland and Midlands provinces in the 1980s. During the 2000 campaigns ZANU-PF would intimidate people saying *tinoisa tsvimbo mugotsi* (they will hit them on the back with a knobkerry) like we did *muhondo* (during the war), meaning they were prepared to beat and kill. They did not have a peaceful strategy fit for modern politics.

With increased economic hardships witnessed from 1990, some urban settlers began to return home because their jobs in the city had been terminated. Usually one was expected to return home to rest, in the sense that when a person died, they would be taken home for burial among *vebwo* (clan descendants). The city was a place of work, entered in search of a living to support the family, while the village was a place of rest and subsistence farming. In the communities under study however, the climate is not so favourable, and farming is done on a low scale because of the erratic rain supply. Returning home after losing a job when someone is still in the economically active group shifted the trajectories of many villagers. For some, the promises of prosperity that were preached by the political elites during rallies were no longer materialising to tangible developments in their lives. The support to cushion the rural populace from severe poverty which had been previously provided by their relatives working in the city had dissipated. Reasons for this decline lay in the political actions of the government, especially corruption scandals, the cost of military action in Matabeleland regions in the 1980s and the civil war in neighbouring Mozambique (1977–1992), as well as the introduction of International Monetary Fund (IMF) backed Economic Adjustment Program (ESAP), and ill-planned government actions in the second decade after independence (Chitiyo 2000; Kairiza 2012).

Even though *sekuru* Dengenya and several participants held the view that those in the village were apolitical because politics was the activity of the elite, I believe that they were always engaged in the political discourse, but may have not recognised their agency in influencing the course of the political game. A game change was necessitated by the socio-economic transformations they witnessed, some of which were dire and personal, giving the political discourse a new impetus, driven by the desire to survive. The resulting tensions in the post-ESAP era were a struggle fought on different grounds (i) an authoritarian regime seeking to retain power and (ii) a wounded citizenry seeking socio-economic liberation. Transitions in this case were rendered by the need for socio-economic and psychosocial liberation, a kind of struggle I believe is transforming the political discourse and could lead to the dismantling of coloniality in Zimbabwe, on the terms of the people and not elites.

Life After ESAP

The introduction of the IMF structural adjustment programmes in the financial year 1991/92 reduced government spending on basic services and reversed or stunted social development among black communities which had been attained in the first decade after independence. For instance, the government made huge budget cuts on healthcare expenditure, which directly impacted the human workforce (Tevera 1997). Between 1991 and 1992, the Ministry of Health and Child Welfare retrenched about 800 health workers and 400 nursing posts were abolished, reducing the workforce by 10% (Osika et al. 2010; Tevera 1997). To this date, the healthcare sector is facing numerous challenges from shortage of skilled healthcare workers to dilapidated and out-dated healthcare infrastructure and shortage of essential medicines and commodities (Mbanje 2018). These challenges have put the sector in a humanitarian crisis, and the healthcare system of Zimbabwe is now mostly supported by donor aid such as the multi-donor Health Development Fund (HDF) and the World Bank RBF scheme (Shava 2016).

A tipping point in the economic meltdown of Zimbabwe was the ill-planned government payouts in August 1997 of an amount of ZWD 50,000 each (approximately USD3000 at the time) to about 60,000 war veterans plus an additional USD125 per month (Chitiyo 2000; Kairiza 2012: 4). Payouts were made to patch relations between the government and war veterans, who had been making demands for compensation and threatening the position of the ruling party (Chitiyo 2000). The government payouts constituted about 3% of the GDP at the time and had significant effect on the budget, which incurred a deficit of 55% (Kairiza 2012: 4). The World Bank responded to the government's spending by temporarily withdrawing a USD62.5 million standing credit line in September until the government had managed to provide a balance of payment plan that could address the deficit (Kairiza 2012: 4). This move worsened tension between the Bretton Woods financial institutions and the Zimbabwean government to this day.

In November 1997, the government made a populist decision to commence plans to compulsorily acquire white-owned commercial farms which created fears among investors and some business owners in the white community (Kairiza 2012). The resulting effect was spontaneous closure and selling of some businesses which prompted the financial crush that occurred on Friday, 14 November 1997, a phenomenon that has been named The Black Friday in Zimbabwe's economic history (Chitiyo 2000; Kairiza 2012). In a single day, the currency markets of Zimbabwe came to a stall, and the Zimbabwean dollar lost value from an exchange rate of ZW$14 to 1US$, to ZW$26:1US$ (Kairiza 2012: 4). This financial crunch rocketed the inflation, and the economy took a downward spiral which it has still not recovered from.

The workers union, Zimbabwe Congress of Trade Union (ZCTU), organised protest actions in January 1998 that disrupted business for two days, posing a threat to the government's hold on power (Chitiyo 2000). Government responded to the protests with a heavy arm and simultaneously introduced price controls to try and cushion the populace (Kairiza 2012: 5). An effect of these price controls was widespread shortages of basic commodities, a feature that recurs presently. Despite the financial challenges facing the country, the late president Mugabe agreed to send a military contingency of 11,000 troops under the SADC protocol in August 1998, to assist the discredited leader of the Democratic Republic of Congo (DRC), fight Rwandan and Ugandan backed rebels (Kairiza 2012: 5). This military intervention has largely been rendered an enrichment exercise by the political elites who had been promised mineral concessions in the DRC (Dietrich 2000). On the contrary, Nest (2001: 470) asserts that President Mugabe as chair of SADC at the time used the intervention to assert his hegemony within the sub-regional bloc and to preserve the integrity of the body. Within a period of two years the military intervention cost the country between USD1.3 million per month in 1998 and USD3 million per month in 1999, it had a delirious effect on the economy (Dietrich 2000; IMF 1999).

Economic hardships and maladministration of state resources throughout the 1990s led to the emergence of a new political party, the Movement for Democratic Change (MDC) in 1999. The MDC gained support from the workers and student union, because its leader, the late Morgan Tsvangirai, had been fighting for workers as the secretary general of the ZCTU. His active lobbying and mobilising within the ZCTU gave his followers confidence for a possible change in governance, because some workers were facing economic hardships due to budget cuts, hyper-inflation and retrenchments. The workers and those under their care were desperate for change, as some stated they 'were tired of having spent 20 years with the same person and their living conditions deteriorating'.

Most of the workers who joined the MDC had connections to their rural homes. *Babamukuru* Mutyairi a 78-year-old man from Buhera stated 'As urban members of the party visited, their relatives, especially in the village, they became ambassadors of the party *kumamisha avo kwavanobva* (village of origin)'. This was feasible because as *vana vebwo* (a child from the village) they were familiar with their communities and knew who to approach and how to approach them. Some of the community members had faced hardships because of ESAP, and this created ripple effects on those supported by their income in the homesteads, for example Mandiza a 40-year-old woman from Buhera stated, 'my father who had been working in Harare told us that *takuvadzwa ne*ESAP *handichakwanisa kukuendesa kuchikoro hupenyu hwakurema* (ESAP has created economic hardships, I can no longer afford to send you to school)'. She was forced to drop out of secondary school in 1995 before completing her Ordinary level studies and had to look for a job as a domestic worker. She moved in with a relative in Gweru (a city 270 km from the capital Harare) and worked as a maid for six years before getting married. When she got married, she moved in with her in-laws in Shurugwi (a town 34 km from Gweru), while her spouse remained working as a taxi driver in Gweru. Their marriage only lasted for three years because her husband was abusive, accused her of being infertile and ended up having extra marital affairs. Since she was married customarily, when the marriage failed, she moved back to her maternal home to take care of the homestead and children of her other siblings.

These deliberations indicated that the economic hardships faced by the working class trickled down to their beneficiaries. Those in the village became aware of the changes happening to their socio-economic environment through the effects experienced by their relatives working in the city. They were no longer passive participants in the political processes shaping the state, but active actors because the actions of the government were shaping their lives in ways that do not fit their aspirations for upward social mobility.

The Voting Curse: 2000–2008

Sekuru Dengenya, indicated that over the period 2000–2008, Buhera became hugely infested with political rivalry and hatred, a phenomenon he had last witnessed during the days of the liberation struggle. Alex Magaisa (2016), a UK-based Zimbabwean lawyer, even dubbed the post-March 2008 electoral violence—an era that 'encapsulates everything that is wrong with elections in Zimbabwe'. The state-sanctioned violence that began in March 2000 targeting white commercial farmers and the rural electorate came as a huge shock to many Zimbabweans.

Talent Helen Mabika, who was petrol, bombed together with Tichaona Chiminya while driving in Buhera during the campaign period in 2000 were among the first victims within the opposition MDC party to be murdered at the hands of the ruling ZANU-PF party (Meldrum 2000b). Arguably, the orchestration of violence against MDC activists in a rural setting was intended to break the emerging backbone of the opposition party, given that the late Morgan Tsvangirai came from Buhera and had been gaining popularity among people from his village area (i.e. Nerutanga and Buhera office) and surrounding. The late Tsvangirai came from Nerutanga village in Buhera, and his family is well respected there. *Babamukuru* Mutyairi described that Tsvangirai's paternal family was based in Nerutanga, but he established his homestead in Makumbe another village in Buhera near the district office, where his mother came from.

Several people from his maternal and paternal side were pleased that '*mwana wekumusha auya nepfungwa yekuti* Buhera *imbotonga nyika*' (a child of the village has come up with the idea of giving Buhera the chance to rule the country). Tsvangirai belongs to the Save clan grouping and the call to bring the seat of government to Buhera, in a way suggested a desire to give rulership to the Dziva clan. Mugabe, who was the incumbent leader, is Gushungo and him being in office for over two decades, in a country that has multiple clan groupings, suggests that he was not only depriving citizens a change in leadership, but blocking other clan groupings from taking the lead. This view raises issues around the socio-genesis of the ideology of tribalism mentioned by Archie Mafeje (1971) that also prevails in Zimbabwe.

In the book '*The Karanga Empire*', Aaron Chigwedere (1985) describes that over 80% of Zimbabwean Africans had a common ancestry and were part of one united political complex up until 1500s. Tribal segmentation and fragmentation occurred around 1700s resulting to multiplicity of clans that were wrongfully labelled as tribes by the colonial administrators. He uses the example that Bantu Africans, had a common ancestry that originated in the Nile valley in north-east Africa and this tribe segmented into three subgroups each with its own identity marks, linked to their totemic values. The creation of ethnolinguistic tribes occurred during the colonial era through the writings of missionaries that had set up religious centres in various parts of the country. For example, American missionaries in the Methodist church took charge of the Manicaland Province and developed the narrative that the Manyika people were distinct from all other Shona people. They created the Manyika tribe, to the extent that by the 1940s people of the Makoni clan who had never been known as Manyika, but as Vaungwe began to refer themselves as Manyika (Chigwedere 1985: 11–12). Similar changes were observed among communities occupied by the Dutch Reformed Church, the Roman Catholics and Salvation Army among others. The ideology of difference along tribal lines is a casualty of the colonial divisionism that occurred, and its effect on the conscience of post-colonial societies in Zimbabwe is the growing lack of tolerance and appreciation of the ethos of life that all humans possess—I am because you are.

Ndlovu-Gatsheni (2015) in the edited volume Mugabeism describes the ideology of tribalism in Zimbabwe as a logic of colonialism that has affected African nationalism and nation-building in several ways. First, it created 'ideological ambivalences, ambiguities and contradictions' that destroyed avenues for formulating an inclusive nation-state in Zimbabwe after attaining independence. Second, it developed a corrupted nationalist identity that was embodied by a few black elites who have continued to advance the logic of colonialism, i.e. divide and rule. What we observe in the nationalist discourse advanced by the ruling elites is a divergence from the African ethos of *hunhuism* and *ukama* (discussed later in the chapter) that enable people to embrace life as a shared enterprise.

State Turns on Its People

The double murders of Chiminya and Mabika (mentioned earlier) in April 2000 coincided with that of David Stevens who was the first white commercial farmer to be murdered by ZANU-PF agents during this election period (Meldrum 2000b). Mr. Stevens was shot in the face on his farm in Marondera by a group of assailants working for ZANU-PF who had tried to invade his farm and were blocked by the farm workers (Meldrum 2000b). The group returned later with more men who opened fire, killing him instantly. About three days from this incident, another farmer Martin Olds was shot dead by suspected ZANU-PF sanctioned elements who had invaded his farm in Nyamandlovu about 80 km from Bulawayo, the second capital (Duval Smith 2000). Mr. Alan Dunn was murdered a few days after the death of Olds at his farm in Beatrice, about 55 km from the capital Harare. Dunn was a local organiser for the MDC who was mobilising support for the party within Beatrice. Six men invaded his farm and lured him outside, where they beat him with chains and sticks and broke chairs over his head as well as smashed him with concrete (Herbert 2000). He later died in the hospital. Mrs. Dunn, in an interview with the Independent UK, shortly after the murder of her husband, stated that the brutal attacks on her spouse were not just about land, but the economy (Herbert 2000).

When the above commercial farmers were attacked, they were asked to confess to 'being members of the MDC' (Meldrum 2000a), which rendered the persons attacking them political agents seeking to reprove opposition. It is highly likely that Dunn and many other white commercial farmers that were targeted during the farm reclamations, were attacked because of alleged (or real) interests in the political activities of the opposition MDC party. These incidents had a huge impact on Zimbabwe's political landscape. Brian Kagoro a human rights defender, speaking to SABC News after the death of Mugabe in September 2019, made remarks that shed light on the economic issue raised by Mrs. Dunn. He argued that Zimbabwe's economy heavily depends on agriculture, and in the early 2000s, the sector employed over 500,000 people, many of them were farm labourers and people of colour. The penetration of the MDC in the white farming community posed a threat to the ruling party because the white farmers were considered conduits for mobilising the black community, (in this case the farm labourers, who in many cases lived with their families and had ties to their home villages), during a time when all other sectors of the economy were already being affected.

However, in the decades prior to 2000, Mugabe's ZANU-PF party had proved capable of using violence to dismantle any elements challenging his seat in government. For instance, in the early 1980s, the infamous Gukurahundi saw Mugabe sanctioning a military force against the late Joshua Nkomo's party, ZAPU and its liberation military wing Zimbabwe People's Revolutionary Army (ZIPRA), on allegations of causing instability in the Matabeleland and Midlands regions of Zimbabwe (CCJP 1997). An estimated 20,000 civilians were murdered and tortured, and many more were displaced. The *Gukurahundi* massacres were initiated by clashes in 1980 at *Entumbane* demobilisation camp in Bulawayo between the former ZANLA—the military wing of ZANU—and ex-ZIPRA combatants—the military wing of ZAPU (CCJP 1997).

Again, in the 1990s Mugabe stifled a new opposition party the Zimbabwe Unity Movement (ZUM), led by Edgar Tekere who was a former member of ZANU-PF (Norman 2015). The resolve of the ruling party when the MDC had successfully mobilised the populace to protest in the late 1990s and to vote against the referendum in 2000 was to unleash violence. The government's response included implementing the brutal fast track land reform (2001–2002), deploying repressive statutory instruments and electoral violence which destroyed spaces for multiparty democracy (Sachikonye 2011). State security agents were deployed to target white farmers (who would potentially sponsor the opposition to defend their investments), the opposition members and rural electorate to disrupt the making of a new political association that could unseat its ruling. These actions caused some Zimbabweans to lose interest and trust in the ruling party, and it also gained enemies in the global arena, particularly Britain the former colonial administrator (Sachikonye 2011).

What made the MDC attractive in the post-2000 was probably that the ruling party no longer fitted the socialist posture it presented during the time of independence (Raftopoulos 2009; Sachikonye 2011). *Babamunini* Mugezo indicated that it became difficult to believe ZANU-PF party's socialist mantra when workers were being retrenched, student loans were being cut off and inflation rising beyond people's earnings. The state had stopped injecting funds to cushion the society from economic hardships because ESAP introduced huge cutbacks and retrenchments. A people's government would have considered alternative ways to avoid retrenchments and cushion its people. But this was not possible because the state was still caught up in what Mignolo (2011) terms the global matrix of coloniality. The Lancaster House deal and the IMF adjustment programmes transposed a Eurocentric governing system that created dependency of the post-colonial state on the colonial administrators. Post-colonial Zimbabwe only gained minimal juridical freedom because liberation movements ascended to political office but remained without the political and economic power needed to position themselves and participate in the global political arena (Ndlovu-Gatsheni 2013). On the contrary, Western powers distanced themselves from the mayhem in Zimbabwe by putting blame on the ruling ZANU-PF for lack of good governance (Kairiza 2012). The ZANU-PF regime continues to accuse the Europe bloc and United States of America for collapsing the economy due to targeted economic sanctions implemented since 2002 (Sachikonye 2011). An effect of the asymmetric global power dynamics at play has been the subversion of hopes and aspirations of the ordinary Zimbabwean by state actors seeking to defend political autonomy.

Reverend Andrianatos speaking at Old's funeral (the commercial farmer from Nyamandlovu mentioned earlier) labelled the late Mugabe a criminal and enemy of the state (APTN Archive Video, Funeral of Slain Farmer Martin Olds, 22/04/2000). This description fits in with the book '*When the State Turns on Its Citizens*', by Brian Sachikonye (2011), who writes that state violence was legitimated to diminish electoral competition and defend the hegemony of the ruling party. Through my research experience and participation in the 2018 harmonised elections in Zimbabwe, I observed that elections have become a vehicle of legitimacy for the ruling ZANU-PF party. Elections have provided legitimacy to politicians, and the ruling ZANU-PF government is deriving its autonomy and monopoly of violence from being elected state actors. Bogaards (2007) who has analysed multiparty elections in 26 African countries (including Zimbabwe) also argues that elections have become instrumental in facilitating transitions towards repressive rule on the continent.

The government has polarised the Zimbabwean society through state security agents and statutory provisions such as the Access to Information and Protection of Privacy Act (AIPPA) of 2002 and the Public Order and Security Act (POSA) of 2002.[2] Another modus operandi used has been to dis-member the citizenry through targeted home raids, beating on the buttocks or head with a heavy object, burning of property or livestock, abductions, unlawful detentions, intimidation and public humiliation at political rallies among others. The recurring feeling of research participants I engaged with in the study was that though they had witnessed violence during the colonial era, they never imagined having to face inhumane atrocities they observed in the years 2000, 2002, 2005 and 2008. The magnitude and spread of violence were highest in 2008. Describing the political environment in Uzumba between 2000 and 2008, *babamunini* Mugezo shared that,

> Violence got physical from as early as 2000. *Hondo yeminda* (farm reclamations) occurred in 2000 to 2002, but never got to the level of the incidents we witnessed in 2008. I know of people who were beaten, some teachers in Uzumba had to flee from as early as 2000 and that fear remained in people. But what occurred in 2008 was extreme, people never thought it would get there.

In the realities of research participants, state-sanctioned violence metamorphosed into a psychosocial state, characterised by fear, disharmony, heartbreak, distrust, resentment and anxiety.

Politics yapinda mumba

Contestations of the two main political parties in Zimbabwe have created tensions among the local community, especially within families and between neighbours, as people are separated in choosing to support the MDC-T or ZANU-PF. *Ambuya* Meso, a widow 48-year-old from Buhera narrated that,

> My husband was sold out by his own blood brother in 2008. *Babamukuru ndivo vakamufumura kumasoja emaguta* (his brother divulged information to the military operatives), who had been hunting down community members suspected of supporting the opposition MDC. When the soldiers came to our house at night, they were accompanied by policemen and ZANU-PF youths who reside in this village.

Research participants described this backstabbing between family or community members using the phrase '*politics yapinda mumba*' (politics has intruded the home). This colloquial expression 'politics *yapinda mumba*' (politics has intruded the home) indicates that political feuds among the elites have increasingly become violent and disruptive to interpersonal relations of families and by extension their cosmological community. The term *mumba* has varying meanings; it can refer to (i) a place of residence or (ii) a family setting (socio-cultural structure of the family). As a place of residence, *mumba* is a private space for living where people resort to and rest after their daily activities.

Mumba can also refer to the socio-cultural structure of families in that people belong to clan groupings that are characterised by an ancestral lineage spanning over generations. These family/clan groupings are identified using totems (Hodzi 1979: 12), which represent the ancestral heritage (family tree) of the given population group. Examples of names of clan groupings in Zimbabwe are *Gumbo* (my own clan name), *Shumba*, *Museyamwa*, *Sinyoro*, *Dziva*, *Murozvi*, *Nyathi*, *Moyo*, *Soko*, *Nzou*, *Kota* and *Tembo*. There are strong socio-cultural ties among clan members across space and time; for example, it is a taboo for people of the same clan name or totem to marry. People maintain family relations through ancestral lineages, inter-clan marriages, common language and a shared living heritage. *Imba* (the family unit) is thus important in the Zimbabwean African setting because everyone comes from a distinct *musha* (place of origin or homestead) and *mhuri* (the family/clan) (Gelfand 1981: 2). These aspects are an important feature in their livelihoods because they draw their identity as *munhu mutema* (black person or African being) from the family, live communally (figuratively and to a greater extent practically) and are related through their clan lines.

Many of the participants in the study self-identify as *munhu mutema* (black person or African being) and subscribe to socio-cultural values, and the African philosophy of *hunhu*. *Munhu mutema* is a loaded term within the Zimbabwean context. First, it is an expression that signifies one's race, i.e. black person, and second, it locates one's ontological and epistemological embodiment, i.e. the African being. This African being should not be viewed as the authentic expression of Africanness because Africa and its people are a product of the interactions that have occurred within the continent and with other civilisations (Mudimbe 1994; Mazrui 2005). What I am discussing is therefore not a romanticised idea that the studied communities have a single factor that makes them uniquely African. Indeed, their identities have been formed out of a combination of complex and overlapping experiences which collectively create synergies and contestations that revere the existence of the social grouping in a spatial locality, geographically located in Africa. Their notion of *munhu mutema* (African being or black person) is an embodiment carved out of complex and coherent forms of existence that oscillate around ideas of *hunhu* (virtues principles) and becoming *munhu ane hunhu* (a virtuous person). Thus, ontologically I am locating the perspectives of the studied population in the African gaze deriving from their socio-cultural values and identity as *vanhu mutema* (African beings).

As *vanhu vatema* (African people), the communities under study, are socialised that *munhu wese ihama* (everyone is family) and *ukama* (family ties) is the foundation of their interpersonal relations (Gelfand 1981: 7). The Shona proverb *matengana gudo* best captures the interconnectedness of the socio-cultural ties that exist among community members which makes everyone family. People belong to clan groupings and are guided to a large extent, by the values and norms of their groupings embodied through the philosophy of *unhu* explained earlier. Social relations are exercised through the positions one holds within the clan, that include being *baba* (father), *amai* (mother), *mbuya* (grandmother), *sekuru* (grandfather or uncle maternal side), *vamwene* (mother-in-law paternal side), *ambuya* (mother-in-law maternal side), *tezvara* (father-in-law), *muroora* (daughter-in-law), *mukwasha* (son-in-law), *mwana* (child), *hanzvadzi* (sibling or cousin), *vatete* (aunt or sister-in-law), *muzukuru* (grandchild), *mainini* (sister-in-law or aunt that is a younger sibling), *babamunini* or *babamudiki* (brother-in-law or uncle that is younger sibling), *babamukuru* (a brother-in-law or uncle that is an older sibling), *maiguru* (sister-in-law or an aunt who is an older sibling), *munin'ina* (younger sibling or cousin) and *mukoma* (older sibling or cousin). Within this family network, figures such as *baba*, *amai*, *mbuya*, *sekuru*, *vamwene*, *ambuya*, *tezvara*, *hanzvadzi*, *vatete*, *mainini*, *babamunini*, *babamukuru*, *maiguru* and *mukoma* command more authority in comparison with the status of *muroora*, *mukwasha*, *mwana*, *muzukuru*. This ordering of the community resonates with the notion of seniority that Oyěwùmí (1997) discusses in her book '*Yoruba's Don't Do Gender*'.

In the Zimbabwean Shona context (here Shona denotes the ethnolinguistic-cultural identity of the studied communities), one's seniority is not absolute. There are two key Shona proverbs that explain the above (i) *mukuru mukuru hanga haigare pfunde* (which contextually instils the idea that each ranking that a person holds earns the individual respect and honour from all) and (ii) *gudo guru peta muswe kuti vadiki vatye* (which means those in senior positions/elderly must respect their juniors/younger persons). These two proverbs embody the mutual respect that is forged among community members because all people have a reciprocal duty to others of upholding *hunhu* regardless of their social position, including their socio-economic status. Hence, the traits *kuzvinipisa* (being humble) and *kuzvibata* (self-discipline) are considered virtuous qualities, in that one needs to always treat others with dignity in order to live in harmony.

Hunhu derived from *unhu* is a spiritual normative framework that locates human beings as interdependent entities who strive to bring the best in society by respecting and valuing the essence of life that all beings possess. *Unhu* as an African embodiment is defined by the traits that one possesses and from these, they attract fortune. A person can have *unhu hwakanaka* (positive traits) or *hwakaipa* (negative traits). But virtuous traits include *kugarisana nevamwe* (living in harmony), *kuzvininipisa* (being humble), *kudyidzana* (friendship or fellowship), *kuzvibata* (self-discipline), *rukudzo* (respect), *kushanda nesimba* (industrious) and *kudzoreka* (teachable spirit), among others.

Both the positive and negative traits attract omen which can make one prosper in life (i.e. good fortune) or encounter misfortunes (possessed by a bad omen). The bad omen is often considered *kuva nemunyama uri kukutevera* (a sense of possession by a bad spirit) that makes everything around you fall apart. The bad omen works as a form of punishment to those who fail to exercise *unhu hwakanaka* (being virtuous). A bad omen travels across space and time; it can cause misfortune to the individual as well as the community. Hence, it is crucial among the local communities to foster virtuous qualities because they contribute to their well-being physically and metaphysically.

Drawing on *ambuya* Meso's encounter, her brother-in-law failed to exercise respect and self-discipline. She indicated that jealousy had made her in-law envious and caused him to disrespect the dignity of his own sibling. This is one of the forms in which political contestations contributed to the decay of interpersonal relations that bind social groupings. The urgent need of the affected communities is to repair relations and to address the bad omen that has been seeded by *ropa rakadeuka* (the blood spilled) during periods of electoral violence.

Political Intrusions and Interpersonal Harms

The late MDC-T leader, Morgan Tsvangirai, considered the state security agents that orchestrated violence between 2000 and 2008 as "well-organised criminals" (AP Archive 2002). This suggests that within the space of high-level political actors, violence was conceived as criminal activity. Mainstream transitional justice discourse regards criminal activity as unlawful conduct that is punishable by a court of law (McEvoy and McConnachie 2013). Many transitional justice initiatives that have treated violence as criminal act tend to focus on prosecuting state actors (as the perpetrator) and individual citizens (as victim), in order to build national cohesion (Lambourne 2009). There are varying sociological and legal definitions that are used to define a victim, victimhood and perpetrator (Girelli 2017).

Proponents of the human rights discourse define a victim as a subject in a conflict situation whose rights have been violated, and the violator is the perpetrator (Girelli 2017; Mamdani 2009). This dichotomy is often used to determine the nature of the criminal offence committed, the applicable laws and this in turn guides the ruling made by the court, which acts as the protector of the violated subject. A key challenge always arises in identifying a victim or perpetrator, regarding whether one or more categories can be used, the criteria to use, and whether the whole community can be entitled the victimhood status. Identifying a victim or perpetrator, therefore, is not only a theoretical problem (Girelli 2017), but practical challenge because of the implications it has on the parties involved in the justice process and the remedy required.

Most transitional communities in Africa have shown that the idea of victim and perpetrator cannot be narrowed down to single individuals because people are the sum of their environment (Mamdani 2009). They are influenced by several factors such as age, gender, religion, sexuality, education, class, ethnicity and culture, among others (Girelli 2017). Moreover, periods of war and conflict tend to not only affect a person directly hurt but everyone else within their vicinity (loved ones) and the broader community. These aspects of humanity influence people's experiences of violence and the version of their past encounters they hold. It is crucial therefore, to have broader understandings of violence, the parties involved, and the remedy required. An alternative approach is to go beyond the concept of rights portrayed in the human rights discourse to the notion of harms (Girelli 2017; Pillsbury 2019; Rubio-Martin and Sandoval 2011). This allows transitional justice initiatives to move beyond addressing the right-holder to incorporate the social tissue and relationships disrupted by violations (Girelli 2017; Mamdani 2009), especially in family settings such as covered in this book. While this shift does not solve the problem of identifying victims and perpetrators in practice, a consideration of harms allows for a broader understanding of the psychosocial effect of violence within a given context. In the rest of the chapter, I adopt an intersectional lens to explore gendered forms of violence experienced by the research participants and its impact on their environments.

Making Meaning of Violence Within Local Context

Participants in the study perceived violence as *mhirizhonga* (violence, instability or disorder), *bopoto* (quarrelling), *kurwisana* (fighting), *makakatanwa* (tensions), *bvongamupopoto* (disruptive behaviour), *bvonga bvonga* (chaos), *nyonganiso* (chaos or disruptions) and *zhowe zhowe* (chaos). These terms capture the harms that occur to relations of the people when violence occurs. Below I unpack the meanings of these terms as described by the research participants.

Mhirizhonga

Mhirizhonga is a form of mayhem or tumultuous behaviour that displaces *runyararo* (peaceful atmosphere) in the community. *Mhirizhonga* can occur in the private spaces of people, for example a homestead being raided by militant operatives, but affects the whole community because of the echoes of the chaotic behaviour displayed in the act of violence. Therefore, it is visible to the public audience within the community because of the loud pronouncements of the chaotic behaviour of parties involved, for example when one is being beaten, they may scream or cry, which travels and alerts the rest of the people in the area. They may not come through to assist the person under attack but will be aware of the chaos they are going through. So even if the outbursts of violence occur in the private space or at night where people are asleep, during daytime conversations about the noise that happened in a homestead spread the news about the incident around the community. This chaotic behaviour destroys the spirit of the community; it causes discomfort and disrupts *kugarisana kwevanhu munharaunda* (living relations of people within the community). *Mai* Mukwa a woman in her early 50s from Mudzi narrated that,

> My son was 20 years old when he was murdered during the post-March 2008 electoral violence. The attack happened towards sunset. He was with a friend when his car was petrol bombed. The two young men

> escaped from the car but my son was already injured and chose to hide behind a nearby bush from the place of the attack. The attackers dragged him from the bush and took him away for further tormenting. His body was discovered after 3 days lying on the side of the road covered in a pool of blood, in a nearby village within the same district. I have been told that some passers-by who first saw his remains had put branches of trees to cover him. His body had been brutally attacked including bullet wounds shot at close range.

This narrative of violence was shared by a mourning mother still grappling to come to terms with the death of her son who was accused of being a sympathizer of the MDC party. Her son was attacked at a shopping centre which is a public space and in full view of the community, but those within vicinity did not take any action to save him. VaMeyiwa a 56-year-old man and close associate to *mai* Mukwa from the same community indicated that though he was not within vicinity when the incident occurred, he got to know of the story through a neighbour who was on the ground when the ordeal happened. I made follow-up engagements with the neighbour, *mai* Chitsi who is a vendor at the township market. She still showed signs of being traumatised by this incident because the young man was her loyal customer, and she also relied on his transport business to ferry her goods around.

Mai Mukwa indicated that she believes her son was murdered for false allegations. In her view, he was an entrepreneur trying to make a living through hiring out his vehicle to community members commuting across the district. Prior to the March 2008 elections, his vehicle had been hired by members of both the ruling ZANU-PF party and the opposition MDC, but when the election results came, and MDC had won seats in constituencies that were previously ZANU-PF strongholds, some members of the ZANU-PF party are said to have conducted a witch hunt of suspected supporters and enablers of the electoral loss. This resulted in her son being publicly terrorised by fellow youths he had trained with in the Border Gezi programme to instil fear and despair in the community. His attackers, the Border Gezi youth militias, are school leavers who went through national youth service training conducted by the government in the early 2000s (Latham 2002). This national youth service programme was intended to empower the youth, instil discipline and impart the nation's values to foster patriotism and youth development. However, those who have taken part in this programme are accused of being indoctrinated with the ZANU-PF political agenda and used as foot soldiers of the party during election periods (Latham 2002).

Bopoto

Bopoto is an argument or *nharo* (quarrelling) that occurs because of difference of opinion. In this context, the difference in opinion is centred around political stances of the ZANU-PF and MDC parties. *Babamukuru* Mutyairi said,

> If you go on social media or public gatherings such as hearings of the NPRC bill you can observe the seeds of hatred on any platforms you join that is discussing Zimbabwean issues. You find that tolerance of differing opinions does not exist. Even if I am not affiliated to any party and I say something that aligns to an idea shared by say ZANU-PF, I am labelled a ruling party member, for example saying that sanctions must go. If also I say something that opposes a person in ZANU-PF, you know how the ruling party has many of its leaders that are accused of causing violence, speaking out on these things one can be labelled an opposition supporter and attacked. It seems there is a template for what one can say and not say, and when you say something contrary you will be considered an opponent.

Bopoto speaks of an absence of tolerance among the warring parties. There might not be any physical violence displayed at the offset, but the lack of tolerance creates divisions. It also adds tension between parties especially when the confrontations involve use of derogatory language. The exchange during *bopoto* is in words used to dehumanise the other, be it in their presence or behind their back. This affects the community because it happens within the visible realm and causes others to take sides, deepening the rift between parties.

Kurwisana

Kurwisana is a state of fighting which can involve physical attacks. It takes the form of continuous battling that can erupt into physical confrontation. For instance, Machonesa, a 63-year-old man from Buhera, stated that,

> When it is election time, we evacuate our homesteads and camp in the mountains because the community will not be safe for us. The village becomes very tense, for example in 2008, we went through troubling times *nekuda kwenyaya dzematongerwo enyika* (due to the political party contestations that were happening in the country).

The MDC and ZANU-PF have been in a state of battle for the past two decades. Their political contestations have created an identity of violence among the party members, where they portray themselves as warriors and foot soldiers of the party. The post-2000 period is considered the Third Chimurenga,[3] which indicates that there is a state of war in Zimbabwe, characterised by a lack of tolerance for political diversity. This war resembles what Achille Mbembe (2019) called the sacrament of democracy in post-colonial Africa that operates by annihilating those regarded enemies of the state. The lack of tolerance in Zimbabwe is displayed in violent reactions that people have on perceived opponents, for example if one wears an MDC t-shirt in an area considered ZANU-PF stronghold, like Uzumba or Mudzi, they will be attacked by elements of ZANU-PF for invading or polluting their territory. So, the violent assaults which are sometimes fatal are displays of allegiance to a political stance, whereby members of the party take a stand to eradicate elements considered to be interfering with their hegemony.

These elements are usually treated as pollutants needing to be fumigated or eradicated. This has led to the emergence of *varakashi* (the beaters) within the ZANU-PF entity who are operatives established to dismantle elements of the opposition MDC or sell-outs. *Varakashi* comes from *kurakasha* which means beating thoroughly or excessively leaving one in a vegetative state. Pollutants are dealt with either overtly (physical attacks) or covertly by being denied access to resources. In rural settings covered in this book, this played out during distribution of aid. Some in the community were denied access to food handouts due to perceived associations with the opposition. Here, traditional authorities within specific villages were key collaborators that often-enabled state actors to deprive some citizens access to resources (Chemhuru 2010). In some instances, they assisted political operatives by giving out information (some of which was false) that put community members in the crossfire. These traditional figures though appointed to represent the clan groupings in each community ended up being re-captured by the ZANU-PF government the same way colonial administrators captured the institution in the colonial era. The logic of colonialism persists through the subjugation of the rural electorate by the dominating party.

Makakatanwa

Makakatanwa is derived from the word *gakava* which is a form of debating that involves putting forward different arguments on a matter. It involves an exchange of words between parties in dispute or deliberation that happens before an audience. *Makakatanwa* can be a positive thing if people have good temperament, they can publicly debate their ideas in a civil manner, giving others room to air their views also. But where there is no tolerance and respect for the difference in opinion among people, it creates tension, because one party may want to dominate the space. Mbata a middle-aged man who attended the public hearings of the NPRC bill in Chinhoyi shared that,

> The atmosphere in this room demonstrates the need for peace and reconciliation. We should not despise the work being done by the government [referring to the peace commission]. We are gathered here to plan together for our future and to ensure that future generations live in a peaceful and prosperous environment. Our parliamentarians should go and represent us when they return to parliament. I think that the president must not be given unrestrained powers to remove the people appointed as commissioners.

His statement was interrupted by ZANU-PF youths in the audience, and they were shouting and threatening to beat him for speaking against the president. They started chanting ZANU-PF slogans and singing '*hatidi zvemadhisinyongoro taramba madhisinyongoro*' (we do not want nonsense, we refuse nonsense). This was about 60–75 minutes into the meeting.

The debating parties such as those in attendance at the NPRC Bill hearings may get aggressive, and the people who suffer most when these platforms become violent, are those who still bare the wounds of the unresolved conflict. What makes these platforms volatile is the lack of tolerance for diverging views. Kuzvi a civil society representative (in his late 30s) at the hearings of NPRC Bill in Harare stated that,

> The sad thing about Zimbabwe is that there is freedom of speech but no freedom after the speech.

This lack of tolerance has been brewed through party indoctrination where the identity of the party becomes the face of the nation, and anything that challenges this synergy is considered an enemy of the state. Terrence Ranger (2004) in the book '*Nationalist Historiography, Patriotic History and the History of the Nation*' has described this as a curse of the patriotic history forged by ZANU-PF nationalists since the dawn of independence. Patriotic history is a restrictive narrative of nationalism that was forged by the ZANU-PF party to dispose parties opposing its rule. This resulted to categorisation of citizens along the binaries of *vana vevhu* (children of the soil) and *vatengesi* (sell-outs). To be regarded *mwana wevhu* (a child of the soil) located one as an authentic citizen with legitimate claim to the state and its resources, while *mutengesi* (a sell-out) was regarded a traitor. These narratives have been shaping the political discourse in the post-2000 era, with ZANU-PF and its supporters presenting themselves as *mwene wevhu* (a figurative for owners of the soil/land and territory). On the contrary, the opposition MDC is depicted as *vadyi vegora* (those who feast on the rot) because they seemed to have the support of actors in the Global North and human rights defenders, and by implication, were polluted elements advancing an agenda of Western governments seeking to topple a 'legitimate' Mugabe/ZANU-PF regime (Ranger 2004; Raftopoulos 2009; Sachikonye 2011).

The interactions between MDC members and ZANU-PF have been confrontational, especially when one considers their political slogans. Chandiwana, a young woman in her 20s, spoke out during the public hearings of the commission in Harare and said,

> The two main political parties in Zimbabwe, ZANU-PF and MDC-T, have political slogans that teach political opponents to be intolerant. ZANU-PF's slogan says *pasi nanhingi* (bring down the individual), which can mean bring that person down six feet under [to the grave]. Similarly, MDC-T goes by the slogan; *isa musoro mudenga, batanidza, rovera pasi* (take it up by the head and slam on the floor). These are directives to do violence.

Many supporters of these parties recite the slogans and arguably take positions without critiquing the images it creates on how they treat someone with a different political position. Worse still, a party that has monopoly of violence usually thrives on *makakatanwa* because it uses the rivalry (uncivil state of debating) to legitimate use of violence to police the population. This control of persons has been occurring with ZANU-PF which silences parties with a divergent view through total subjugation to the views of the domineering party.

Bvongamupopoto

Bvongamupopoto is made up of two words (i) *bvonga*—an act of mixing elements or creating confusion—and (ii) *mupopoto*—derived from the word *bopoto* which means an argument or quarrel. These words combined define a state of disagreement that amounts to chaotic behaviour which disrupts *runyararo* (peace). *Bvongamupopoto* is an escalation of *bopoto* which manifests itself as *bvonga bvonga* explained below.

Bvonga bvonga

Bvonga bvonga derives from *kubvonyonga* which means *kunyanganisa zvinhu zvekuti zvinoshaya chimiro* (a state of confusion or commotion). It can also be understood as *kuvhiringidza* (disrupting something). *Bvonga bvonga* is therefore an act or actions that cause disharmony in society by breaking the bond of trust that holds communities together. One may wonder whether trust ever really existed in the studied communities. There is no straightforward answer to this, but one can deduce that from their notion of *ukama* (family ties), there are elements of cohesion and cooperation that exists which are forged by the understanding that they are all *vanhu veukama* (related people). These relations have a functional value in how people treat each other, and their respect for one another is channelled through their clan grouping ties.

Hence, you can observe that when the people meet for the first time, they raise the questions: (i) *munobva kupi* (which village do you come from) and (ii) *munoerei* (what is your totem)? Once one's African roots have been located (i.e. through name of village and clan name), they start calling each other by their clan praise name, for instance Save, Madyira, Museyamwa and Chirandu. These relations forge bonds that bring people together even though they live in different villages. They can be scarred when one betrays the trust and respect earned from their *ukama* (family ties). For example, *babamunini* Mugezo's ordeal in 2008 was sanctioned by a fellow community member, someone he considered *mukoma* (big brother). He shared that,

> The guy who organised my attack in April 2008 was outspoken at several rallies that were organised in our area before the June run-off election. He boasted that he was going to deal with any other element in our area who they find working with the opposition, the same way they dealt with me. Even though the accusations were fabricated because I had never attended any meeting of the opposition, my attack was well-planned to break my spirit. Being spoken of at political rallies shows that *tanga tave munguva yemhirizhonga nekuti munhu chaiye haangafare nekurohwa kana kukuvara kweumwe* (we were living in a state of mayhem because it is not humane for someone to find pleasure in the beatings or harm faced by others).

The phrase *munhu chaiye* stated by *babamunini* Mugezo in the above narrative poses a question on the humanity of persons within the African setting. In the Zimbabwean Shona etiology, *munhu* (the being) becomes a being when they have *unhu* (virtuous qualities) because life is a shared enterprise (*munhu vanhu*). The functional value of *hunhu* is grounded in a person's ability to be *munhu ane hunhu* (depicting qualities of hunhu). The man described by *babamunini* Mugezo lacked *hunhu* because he did not exercise *kugarisana nevamwe* (living in harmony), *kuzvininipisa* (being humble), *kudyidzana kwakanaka* (good friendship or fellowship) and *kuzvidzora* (self-restraint). His actions damaged relations of community members because he was terrorising people for political gain.

Nyonganiso

Nyonganiso is an act of *kupesanisa vanhu* which means putting people against each other and tearing relations. Mandiza, a 63-year-old man from Buhera, related that,

> It should not be a crime in this country for one to choose a political party to support because our constitution recognizes the state as a multi-party democracy. However, when you look within a family/clan, siblings and relatives will not be in good relations due to political party contestations. Some might belong to ZANU-PF and others MDC, such that when it comes to elections those belonging to ZANU-PF are used by their party leaders to divulge information about who in their family is supporting the opposition. Those affiliated with the opposition are then hunted down and dealt with.

Another participant Mandidirei a 51-year-old woman from the same community said,

> The police would arrest people who were listed on the wanted people's list and submit them to the soldiers who had set up a military base here to discipline MDC-T supporters.

The soldiers mentioned by Mandidirei were rogue military personnel collaborating with a youth militia that had been carefully created to service interests of the ruling party. *Babamunini* Mugezo explained these elements by stating that,

> *Pakatanga kurohwa vanhu* (when the violent attacks started) in April 2008, a military operative the Joint Operation Command (JOC) had already set up structures in the community. *Munhu ane* rank yacommander (a person with the rank of commander) and above within the JOC and above was deployed in the district charged to set up camps or bases from where they mobilised the youths to go out and beat, kill or terrorise opposition members and any suspected affiliates. The youths would be assembled every day and given propaganda and education on how to operate when raiding their target subject. There were other members of the army *vakangonyuka* (who just surfaced in the community). During the day some of the elements would travel from place to place conducting rallies and intimidating people, *vaizotaura nemayouth* (they would gather the youths) and give them methods of operation. At night they would target their victims, beat them up, commit acts of arson, murder and rape also. All operations were done during the night. There was no violence during the day, it was quiet, if there were rallies, they appeared to be normal but with threats. During the night they would do the raids, i.e. going to someone who is unsuspecting and cause harm.

The youths that were used to commit acts of violence were members of the same community who knew the people they were attacking. Various reasons could be drawn up to explain the capture of the youths into acts of terror by state elements, for example the plight of poverty and high youth unemployment (*Human Rights Watch* 2008), but it remains key to observe that they too were victims of violence. This links back to the debate of challenges around defining victims and perpetrators, especially in a context where acts of violence were done largely out of cohesion or a belief in an eminent threat that needed to be dealt with. Here, the cohesion makes provision for those who acted under duress, which some in the community argued was an issue that forced the youths to attack their loved ones, in fear of being attacked. For example, the murder of *mai* Mukwa's son by youths from his own community he had been peers with, she explained this as acts that were done under duress. In her case, though she was disappointed by the behaviour of her son's peers, her anger and hurt was directed more towards the political figures who ordered these youths, who were also fellow community members. Since the ruling party had created the narrative that the MDC were sell-outs requiring to be uprooted from the community, *Babamunini* Mugezo commented that their acts of terror may have been a display of bravery and to gain recognition for defending the party.

In the post-2000 era, there were several jingles composed to advance the ZANU-PF party's war mantra, such as *Zimbabwe Ndeye Ropa* (loosely translating to Zimbabwe was birthed through sacrifices), which encouraged party members to take all measures to defend *ivhu* (the land/state) including spilling blood of any perceived threat to the state/ZANU-PF (Raftopoulos 2009). The binary between the state and the party was conflated to advance a nationalist discourse centred around ZANU-PF and its legitimacy to the land and defending the territory. Losing the first round of the 2008 presidential elections was considered a close call on Mugabe/ZANU-PF, that needed to be rectified by ensuring that the assumed defectors vote properly in the run-off; hence, the post-March violent attacks were dubbed Operation *Mavhotera Papi* (Where did you cast your vote?) (*Human Rights Watch* 2008). Several research participants in Buhera who come from the same village or neighbouring villages to Morgan Tsvangirai's homestead mentioned that they were attacked because of the ties they have with the Tsvangirai family. They further suggested that the victimisation of community members was conducted systematically, making use of underground informants and insiders who spied on people. These acts of spying and violent attacks were arguably necessary sacrifices to defend the state for political gain. However, it has destroyed *hushamwari* (friendships), *ukama* (family ties) and *kudyidzana kwevanhu* (fellowship) in the community, which makes the underlying fabric that holds communities together and foster harmony.

Zhowe zhowe

Zhowe zhowe describes an element of group behaviour that manifests as tensions or chaos causing rifts and instability in the community. For example, when people were attacked in their homesteads, the assailants often came as a mob and their group behaviour was disruptive to all spaces they passed. The display of violence within the community created fear, anxiety and silenced communities from castigating the actors because the mob would be uncontrollable. The assailants demonstrated a lack of self-restraint and operating like a veld fire or lose lion seeking to devour anything in its path.

Conclusion

When violence occurs in the life world of the studied communities, it does not only affect the individual, but destroys the network of relations that exist among people which makes their social fabric. Participants in this study believe that a living being is a spirit being, who belongs to a cosmological community made up of the physical and metaphysical realms. Within each realm are living entities bound by an interdependent relationship that connects those existing in the physical world and the metaphysical through *ukama*. Justice is therefore not a mechanism, but a process aimed at repairing the relational harms and diffusing the bad omen that comes from *unhu hwakaipa* (bad behaviour), in order to sustain a harmonious relation between entities in both the physical and metaphysical realms. Understanding these cosmologies broadens our conception of violence, peace and justice by making room for the humanistic and spiritual values of African communities. It provides for acknowledgement of who we are as individuals, a community and the society. This in turn helps to depict the disruptions of violence on the human being and community in which they exist (made up of the physical and cosmological/metaphysical realms), as well as capture how peace and justice manifests.

A state-centric approach would overlook these effects of violence on the interpersonal relations, ties, values and norms that bind people in the local communities under study. Therefore, a turn to the local, which I regard as a standpoint that is based in locality but not bound by it (Sharp 2014; Shaw et al. 2010), provides a shifted vantage point. It allows people to recognise local communities as sites of knowledge and platforms for justice processes that are informed by the lived experiences of the people.

Notes

1. Second Chimurenga refers to the liberation struggle fought between 1965 and 1979 between black nationalist movements, ZAPU and ZANU-PF, against the Rhodesian government under Ian Smith. A British-led mediation process at Lancaster House, London, in 1979 brought the warring parties together—the Patriotic Front, represented by Joshua Nkomo and Robert Mugabe, and the Rhodesian government represented by Ian Smith and Bishop Abel Muzorewa—to forge a settlement, the Lancaster House Agreement (Mlambo 2014).
2. A precursor to POSA was the Law Order and Maintenance Act (LOMA) of 1960 created by the Rhodesian government to control the populace (Sachikonye 2011). The POSA statute implemented in 2002 has been used to prevent civilians, opposition political actors and the civil society from holding public gatherings and to freely deliberate on political issues in the country. While AIPPA has censored the media, particularly between 2002 and 2008, such that citizens could not get any news criticizing current affairs in the country from privately owned local media houses (Raftopoulos 2009). Failure to comply with the above statutes resulted to state punishment with penalties such as fines and imprisonment.
3. Third Chimurenga or *Hondo Yeminda* is the term used to refer to violent campaigns led by war veterans and ZANU-PF security agents witnessed in the post-2000 period. It began in 2000 with the violent reclamation of farming land owned by white farmers which were backed by the government's fast-track land reform program. In the same era, members of the newly created MDC party were targeted as sell outs working with white farmers and Western governments to advance imperialist agenda since the government had been put under economic sanctions by the European bloc for human rights violations associated with the land reclaims and electoral violence (Kriger 2003; Ndlovu-Gatsheni 2011).

References

AP Archive. 2002. *Opposition Leader Visits Family of Murdered Supporter*. Available from http://www.aparchive.com/metadata/Zimbabwe-Tsvangirai/. Accessed 2 December 2019.

APTN Archive. 2000. *Funeral of Slain Farmer Martin Olds*. Available from http://www.aparchive.com/metadata/ZIMBABWE-FUNERAL-OF-SLAIN-FARMER-MARTIN-OLDS/. Accessed 2 December 2019.

Bogaards, M. 2007. Measuring Democracy Through Election Outcomes: A Critique with African Data. *Comparative Political Studies* 40 (10): 1211–1237.

Catholic Commission for Justice, Peace in Zimbabwe and Legal Resources Foundation (Zimbabwe). 1997. Breaking the Silence, Building True Peace: A Report on the Disturbances in Matabeleland and the Midlands, 1980 to 1988. Catholic Commission for Justice and Peace in Zimbabwe.

Chemhuru, M. 2010. Democracy and the Paradox of Zimbabwe: Lessons from Traditional Systems of Governance. *The Journal of Pan African Studies* 3 (10): 180–191.

Chigwedere, A. 1985. *The Karanga Empire*. Harare: Books for Africa.

Chitiyo, T.K. 2000. Land, Violence and Compensation: Reconceptualising Zimbabwe's Land and War Veterans Debate. *Track Two* 3: 25.

De Sousa Santos, B. (ed.). 2007. *Cognitive Justice in a Global World: Prudent Knowledges for a Decent Life*. Lanham: Lexington Books.

Dietrich, C. 2000. The Commercialisation of Military Deployment in Africa. *African Security Review* 9 (1): 3–17.

Duval Smith, A. 2000. *Butchered by a Mob, His Only Crime Was to Be White Farmer in Mugabe's Zimbabwe*. Available from https://www.independent.co.uk/news/world/africa/butchered-by-a-mob-his-only-crime-was-to-be-a-white-farmer-in-mugabes-zimbabwe-282172.html. Accessed 23 September 2019.

Edwards, G., and C. Tisdell. 1989. The Educational System of Zimbabwe Compared with Those of Selected African and Advanced Countries: Costs, Efficiency and Other Characteristics. *Comparative Education* 25 (1): 57–76.

Gelfand, M. 1981. *Ukama*. Gwelo: Mambo Press.

Girelli, G. 2017. *Understanding Transitional Justice: A Struggle for Peace, Reconciliation and Rebuilding*. Cham: Palgrave Macmillan.

Herbert, R. 2000. *Widow: 'Farm Murder Was Political'.* Available from https://www.independent.co.uk/news/world/africa/widow-farm-murder-was-political-276331.html. Accessed 9 September 2019.

Hodzi, A.C. 1979. *Shona Praise Poetry*. Oxford: Clarendon Press.

Human Rights Watch. 2008. *"Bullets for Each of You": State Sponsored Violence Since Zimbabwe's March 29 Elections.* Available from https://www.hrw.org/report/2008/06/09/bullets-each-you/state-sponsored-violence-zimbabwes-march-29-elections. Accessed 17 August 2019.

IMF. 1999. *Zimbabwe Letter of Intent, July 16*. Available from https://www.imf.org/external/np/loi/1999/071699.htm. Accessed 14 August 2019.

Kairiza, T. 2012. Unbundling Zimbabwe's Journey to Hyperinflation and Official Dollarization. GRIPS. Policy Information Center. Discussion Paper: 09–12.

Kanyongo, G.Y. 2005. Zimbabwe's Public Education System Reforms: Successes and Challenges. *International Education Journal* 6 (1): 65–74.

Kriger, N. 1991. *Zimbabwe's Guerrilla War: Peasant Voices.* Cambridge: Cambridge University Press.

Kriger, N. 2003. *Guerrilla Veterans in Post-War Zimbabwe: Symbolic and Violent Politics, 1980–1987*. Cambridge: Cambridge University Press.

Lambourne, W. 2009. Transitional Justice and Peacebuilding After Mass Violence. *International Journal of Transitional Justice* 3 (1): 28–48.

Latham, B. 2002. *Mugabe Trains 100,000 Thugs to Spread Terror*. Available from https://www.telegraph.co.uk/news/worldnews/africaandindianocean/zimbabwe/1381351/Mugabe-trains-100000-thugs-to-spread-terror.html. Accessed 18 June 2019.

Mafeje, A. 1971. The Ideology of 'Tribalism'. *The Journal of Modern African Studies* 9 (2): 253–261.

Magaisa, A. 2016. *The Big Saturday Read: Remembering 27 June—Probably the Darkest Chapter in Zimbabwe's Electoral History.* Available from https://www.bigsr.co.uk/single-post/2016/07/02/The-Big-Saturday-Read-Remembering-27-June-%E2%88%92-probably-the-darkest-chapter-in-Zimbabwe%E2%80%99s-electoral-history. Accessed 29 October 2019.

Maldonado-Torres, N. 2007. On the Coloniality of Being. *Cultural Studies* 21 (2, 3): 240–270.

Mamdani, M. 1996. *Citizen and Subject: Contemporary Africa and the Legacy of Late Colonialism.* Princeton, NJ: Princeton University Press.

Mamdani, M. 2009. Response by Mahmood Mamdani. *International Journal of Transitional Justice* 3 (3): 470–473.

Mashingaidze, T.M. 2010. Zimbabwe's Illusive National Healing and Reconciliation Processes: From Independence to the Inclusive Government 1980–2009. *Conflict Trends* 2010 (1): 19–27.

Mazrui, A. 2005. The Re-invention of Africa: Edward Said, V. Y. Mudimbe, and Beyond. *Research in African Literatures* 36 (3): 68–82.

Mbanje, P. 2018. *Maternal Deaths Still a Headache*. Available from https://www.newsday.co.zw/2018/10/maternal-deaths-still-a-headache/. Accessed 16 June 2019.

Mbembe, A. 2019. *Necro-Politics*. Durham: Duke University Press.

McEvoy, K., and K. McConnachie. 2013. Victims and Transitional Justice: Voice, Agency and Blame. *Social & Legal Studies* 22 (4): 489–513.

Meldrum, A. 2000a. *Opposition Reports New Attacks as White Farm Owner Killed*. Available from https://www.irishtimes.com/news/opposition-reports-new-attacks-as-white-farm-owner-killed-1.268835. Accessed 2 December 2019.

Meldrum, A. 2000b. *They Kept Saying We Were Going to Die*. Available from https://www.theguardian.com/world/2000/apr/17/zimbabwe.andrewmeldrum. Accessed 2 December 2019.

Mignolo, W. 2011. *The Darker Side of Western Modernity: Global Futures, Decolonial Options*. Durham and London: Duke University Press.

Mlambo, A.S. 2014. *A History of Zimbabwe*. Cambridge: Cambridge University Press.

Mudimbe, V.Y. 1994. *The Idea of Africa*. Oxford: James Currey.

Ndlovu-Gatsheni, S.J. 2009. *Do 'Zimbabweans' Exist? Trajectories of Nationalism, National Identity Formation and Crisis in a Postcolonial State*, vol. 3. Oxford: Peter Lang.

Ndlovu-Gatsheni, S.J. 2011. The Construction and Decline of Chimurenga Monologue in Zimbabwe: A Study in Resilience of Ideology and Limits of Alternatives. Comparative Perspectives from East and Southern Africa paper presented at the 4th European Conference on African Studies (ECAS4), Nordic Africa Institute, June 15–18, Uppsala.

Ndlovu-Gatsheni, S.J. 2013. The Entrapment of Africa Within the Global Colonial Matrices of Power: Eurocentrism, Coloniality, and Deimperialization in the Twenty-First Century. *Journal of Developing Societies* 29 (4): 331–353.

Ndlovu-Gatsheni, S.J. (ed.). 2015. *Mugabeism? History, Politics, and Power in Zimbabwe*. New York: Palgrave Macmillan.

Nest, M. 2001. Ambitions, Profits and Loss: Zimbabwean Economic Involvement in the Democratic Republic of the Congo. *African Affairs* 100 (400): 469–490.

Norman, A. 2015. *Robert Mugabe and the Betrayal of Zimbabwe*. Jefferson, NC: Mc Farland & Company Inc.

Nyere, C. 2016. The Continuum of Political Violence in Zimbabwe. *Journal of Social Sciences* 48 (1, 2): 94–107.

Osika, J., D. Altman, L. Ekbladh, H. Nguyen, T.W. Rosenfeld, and S. Tapera. 2010. *Zimbabwe Health System Assessment 2010*. Bethesda, MD: Health Systems 20/20 Project, Abt Associates Inc.

Oyěwùmí, O. 1997. *The Invention of Women: Making and African Sense of Western Gender Discourse*. Minneapolis: University of Minnesota Press.

Pillsbury, S.H. 2019. What Is Relational Justice? Loyola Law School, Los Angeles Legal Studies Research Paper No. 2019-09. Available from https://ssrn.com/abstract=3338052. Accessed 30 November 2019.

Quijano, A. 2000. Coloniality of Power and Eurocentrism in Latin America. *International Sociology* 15 (2): 215–232.

Quijano, A. 2007. Coloniality and Modernity/Rationality. *Cultural Studies* 21 (2–3): 168–178.

Raftopoulos, B. 2009. The Crisis in Zimbabwe, 1998–2008. In *Becoming Zimbabwe. A History from the Pre-colonial Period to 2008: A History from the Pre-colonial Period to 2008*, ed. B. Raftopoulos and A. Mlambo, 201–232. Avondale, Harare: African Books Collective.

Ranger, T. 1967. *Revolt in Southern Rhodesia, 1896–7: A Study in African resistance*. London: Heinemann.

Ranger, T. 2004. Nationalist Historiography, Patriotic History and the History of the Nation: The Struggle Over the Past in Zimbabwe. *Journal of Southern African Studies* 30 (2): 215–234.

Rubio-Martin, R., and C. Sandoval. 2011. Engendering the Reparations Jurisprudence of the Inter-American Court of Human Rights: The Promise of the Cotton Field Judgment. *Human Rights Quarterly* 33 (4): 1062–1091.

SABC Digital News. 2019. *Reflecting on Mugabe's Legacy with Brian Kagoro*. Available from https://www.youtube.com/watch?v=mqdSwsIW1Zs. Accessed 1 October 2019.

Sachikonye, L. 2011. *When a State Turns on Its Citizens: 60 Years of Institutionalised Violence in Zimbabwe*. Oxford: African Books Collective.

Sharp, D.N. 2014. Addressing Dilemmas of the Global and the Local in Transitional Justice. *Emory International Law Review* 29 (1): 71–117.

Shava T. 2016. *Donor-Driven Health Fund Reviving Zimbabwe Health Sector*. Available from https://www.voazimbabwe.com/a/donor-driven-health-fund-reviving-zimbabwe-health-sector/3301830.html. Accessed 16 May 2019.

Shaw, R., L. Waldorf, and P. Hazan. 2010. *Localizing Transitional Justice: Interventions and Priorities After Mass Violence*. Stanford, CA: Stanford University Press.

Tevera, D. 1997. Structural Adjustment and Health Care in Zimbabwe. In *Issues and Perspectives on Health Care in Contemporary Sub-Saharan Africa*, ed. E. Kalipeni and P. Thiuri, 227–242. Lewiston, NY: The Edwin Mellen Press.

3

Harm, Displacement and Interpersonal Justice

Abstract While the National Peace and Reconciliation Commission Bill provides a legal framework on which transitional justice processes in Zimbabwe can occur, it remains limited because it is an elitist project seeking to provide national cohesion. On the contrary, transitional justice as imagined in this chapter is a social process for repairing relational harms among community members in a cosmological way. The chapter draws on the life history of *babamunini* Mugezo from Uzumba who was affected by political violence in 2008 to establish the local processes of justice employed to remedy his encounters. I establish that interpersonal justice is an active continuous process geared at renewing the essence of humanity through upholding socio-cultural values of African beings enshrined in *Hunhuism.*

Keywords Life history · Hunhu · *Dare* · Interpersonal justice · Cosmic balance · Renewal · Essence of humanity

R. Murambadoro, *Transitional Justice in Africa*,
Development, Justice and Citizenship,
https://doi.org/10.1007/978-3-030-48092-9_3

Introduction

It has been over a decade since Zimbabweans witnessed the unprecedented state-sanctioned violence that accompanied the post-March 2008 elections. Many people were injured, displaced and murdered, which forced some to flee their homes to neighbouring towns or further afar in the diaspora. *Babamunini* Mugezo is one of those who went into exile and despite the establishment of the National Peace and Reconciliation Commission (NPRC) in 2018 to attend to past injustices or a military assisted change of government in 2017,[1] he does not feel 'safe' to come back to his home country. This chapter focuses on the life history of *babamunini* Mugezo to establish the violence that has accompanied his trajectory and the avenues he has pursued to find healing.

Life Before the Attack

Babamunini Mugezo was born and raised in Uzumba in the late 1960s; he is the eldest surviving child in a family of 13 siblings. He attended his primary education in the same district, at Musanhi primary, this was during the time of the liberation struggle. His family was moved into the protected villages that were set up by the Rhodesian government and he lived there for about two years, 1975–1977. Though they had been displaced from their homes and moved to temporary shelter, the violence did not stop. On several occasions, guerrilla fighters attacked the protected villages and burned down their shelters. When the guerrilla fighters raided a protected village, they often abducted people to join them. The first KEEP he witnessed being burned was in August 1977. Some of the villagers when they escaped the invasions, they were accommodated by freedom fighters in nearby mountains and were indoctrinated on the liberation discourse.

In his view, collaboration with the guerrillas became an essential means for villagers to avoid being targeted unaware. Sometimes before a village was attacked people would have been informed through informants about the targeted area. They prepared for the attack by smuggling out their belongings into the nearby fields. When the attack occurred, they would have little to carry as they ran away into hiding. *Babamunini* Mugezo left Uzumba temporarily in December 1977 because his family had been warned about plans of some guerrilla fighters to extinguish members of his household. He shared that,

> some of the villagers from our KEEP had been abducted and taken to the camps of ZANLA militants. They divulged information about my father's employment. He was a police officer in the Rhodesian government.

His family was targeted for attacks by the ZANLA forces because his father vaChibundwa was considered an enemy of the struggle. The father was based in Beitbridge at the time, and out of fear his family relocated and joined him. A few months later in 1978 the protected villages were abolished, and people moved back to their homes, and they also moved back to Uzumba. He completed his secondary education in the late 1980s and went on to qualify as a secondary school teacher. After obtaining his diploma from Gweru Teachers' College (now Midlands State University) he returned to work in Uzumba.

At the time he returned to work in Uzumba in the early 1990s, his uncle called Nyangwe was in a relationship with a white woman Madam Cathy who lectured at a nearby mission school. He became friends with his uncle's partner especially because they had a common interest in English literature. The two would occasionally hang out at the local bottle store together with his uncle and since Madam Cathy was mobile, they sometimes went to other places out of Uzumba. During their expeditions they would discuss different English literature set books being taught in their schools. Two books that he enjoyed the most were *'Harvest of Thorns'* by Shimmer Chinodya (1990) and George Orwell's (1946) *'Animal Farm'*. In this era, the Zimbabwean Ordinary Level English literature syllabus was divided into three sections that covered African literature, English literature and poetry and play. An English literature teacher could choose to teach two-set books each from African and English literature, or one set book and combine with poetry and play. In his case he chose two-set books *Harvest of Thorns* (under African literature) and *Animal Farm* (English literature), but also taught the play Romeo and Juliet.

The combination of *Harvest of Thorns* and *Animal Farm* was important for him because of thematic similarities. He shared that,

> *Harvest of Thorns* is a literary non-fiction book based on a Zimbabwean setting during the colonial and post-colonial period. It revolves around a character called Benjamin who was born under the colonial regime and ended up joining the liberation struggle to fight the removal of the white government. He came back from war when Zimbabwe gained independence but had sustained injuries that left him disabled. After independence Benjamin lived in Mbare, on the outskirts of the city and his sufferings remained the same, if not worse since he was now unemployable. Hence the book title suggested that Benjamin's liberation efforts had only beget the same predicaments.

Considerably, a similarity of this set book with *Animal Farm* is the continuation of strife in lives of the masses under leaders brought in through people's revolution. *Animal Farm* is a satiric set book with a European setting. It is based on the Russian Revolution of 1917, where the peasants and working class toppled the Tsar of Russia Nicholas II, led by Vladimir Lenin who went on to become leader of the Soviet Union. However, the living conditions of the peasants and working class in the Soviet Union remained unchanged, which led to continued strife between the government and masses.

The two-set books provided converging points for discussion between *babamunini* Mugezo and Madam Cathy with regard to issues of power struggles, race relations, social inequality and disparities facing the Zimbabwean post-colonial society. They also discussed Freedom Nyamubaya's (1995) book *Dusk of Dawn*, though it was not a set book. Nyamubaya was born in Uzumba like *babamunini* Mugezo, and she joined the ZANLA forces during the liberation struggle. In her book, which is a collection of short stories and poems, she discusses that despite the attainment of independence, the country is still divided by race, gender, ethnicity and social class. The recurring theme in these three books in relation to Zimbabwe was the issue that coloniality still endured and is embodied by the black elites who took over from the white colonialists. These set books enabled them to engage on political issues of the day without necessarily becoming antagonistic to each other.

In 2001 when the economic situation in Zimbabwe had turned for the worst, *babamunini* Mugezo registered for a bachelors' degree in Media studies with the Zimbabwe Open University (ZOU). He shared that,

> From 2001 I had started a degree in Media Studies, and I learned things like news and propaganda. Because of my studies I had to read both the public and private media. So, as I read newspapers some people in the community would see me or even ask about the stories covered. Most of my reading material came from Harare because there was a bus driver, I knew who would bring me newspapers every day. I kept most of the newspapers in my office because I often used it as my study room. Reading both private and public media was important for comparative purposes as a Media student.

Newspapers in the village are often used as toilet paper. As such some community members were eager to collect newspapers from *babamunini* Mugezo when he had finished reading for domestic use. He became a reliable supplier of the much-needed free toilet paper, but also interpreter of the contents of the newspapers to the few people he discussed with.

At the time of his studies he became a senior teacher of his school and was assigned the duty of liaising with parents on student affairs. His school had boarding facilities and often parents would come to visit their children but when they came out of the visiting hours, they needed permission from the senior teacher in charge. As a resident teacher parents frequented his house. He shared that, 'some people seeing from the community would ask why I get frequent visitors from Harare with cars?'

This raised suspicions about his associations, especially in an era where the opposition had been making inroads through interactions between people in the city and the village. Harare was considered the base of the opposition MDC and those from the city were assumed to be supporters of the opposition. Hence the frequent home visits by parents, who were assumed to be coming from Harare, made some in his community concerned about his political affiliation since the emergence of MDC. These suspicions were compounded by his absence from political meetings organised in his community, which made some to conclude that he was a member of the opposition. However, he explained that,

> I frequented Harare when I started my studies for classes and would go fortnightly. Some thought I was going for meetings in Harare. They never asked what sent me to Harare. So, it got to a point that let's say a rally is conducted on Friday or over weekend and I would not be available, they took offence. Uzumba *ndiko kumusha* (is my village of origin) my home was 10 km from my school. People expected me to participate in local politics and my absence was regarded a deliberate act of defiance. There were some people in the community who were tired of attending rallies, so they did not go, but that was not the case with me. Consequences of not attending rallies after 2000 were heavily noticeable, for instance the community leaders would deliberately omit your name from the food aid distribution list.

Thus, his absence from political meetings and frequent association with parents from Harare brewed suspicions of him being an MDC agent. These suspicions grew even more when he was involved in the teachers' union and later appointed an official for the Zimbabwe Electoral Commission (ZEC) in his region, as discussed in the next section.

Becoming a Stranger in Your Own Home

In our series of interviews held in 2019, *babamunini* Mugezo indicated that he believes he was attacked in the post-March 2008 election violence because of his involvement in elections as an official for the ZEC. He was attacked during the three months of terror (April–June 2008) that have been colloquially dubbed *Operation Makavhotera Papi (Where did you put your vote?)*. This term refers to the brutal attacks that were unleashed by operatives allegedly sanctioned by the ruling ZANU-PF party on suspected supporters and members of the opposition party MDC across the country. A Human Rights Watch (2008) report titled '*Bullets for Each of You*' described the post-March 2008 electoral violence as a campaign that was forged by the ruling ZANU-PF party to destroy political opposition and ensure Mugabe's victory in the presidential run-off that was set for 27 June 2008. Acts of terror witnessed in this period have rendered the year 2008 one of the darkest moments in the history of post-colonial Zimbabwe, although *Gukurahundi* which occurred in the early 1980s remains the deadliest, especially in terms of fatalities and scale of violations.

He believes that another community member who was a teacher and local council chair, Mairasa, fabricated the information that contributed to his attack. The two had known each other from a young age, they attended secondary school together. *Babamunini* Mugezo passed his secondary education on time and processed to teacher training, while Mairasa remained behind and repeated his O'levels. Mairasa later trained to be a teacher but was actively involved in the ZANU-PF party. As former schoolmates and fellow community members, he considered him a brother, especially because they had kinship ties.

One day in early 2008 another friend of his who knew both parties informed him of a conversation he had overheard in a bottle store at the shopping centre, where Mairasa was tarnishing his image calling him an MDC agent. Given the polarisation of his community, such accusations were deadly. *Babamunini* Mugezo confronted Mairasa about the allegations. It emerged that some community members had been monitoring his movements, especially that he often visited a building at Murehwa shopping centre that was known to belong to an MDC member. He described his shocking discovery saying,

> The said building had two floors, the ground floor was used as a supermarket, there was also a bank and a few other stores. On the second floor there were many rooms mostly used as offices by different organisations, for instance the Zimbabwe Teachers' Association Co-operative Credit Union (ZCCU) had an office there. I was part of a housing cooperative, DESTINY of Africa Network (DANet), which was housed in the same building. I was a chairperson[2] of its chapter in our area. As a cooperative we employed a clerk who sat in this building hence my frequent visits. I would go at least once a week to have meetings and address issues such as going to the council to apply for land. So Mairasa knew about the cooperative because he was a council chair and a teacher also. It came to me as a shock that false information was being spread about my association with the occupants in the building. I believe some teachers with political connections had wanted houses through the cooperative but were unable to get them, which made them jealous.

Having dealt with his former schoolmate he thought the rumours would disappear and not amount to any harm on him. However, he received information from another colleague about an eminent attack planned for him and was advised to run away. Instead of fleeing he approached the military operative, Muchandiona, who had been mentioned as the commander plotting his attack, since he knew him as a friend to his cousin Reason. Muchandiona professed in his face that nothing bad had been said against him. The two parties engaged about the contributions *babamunini* Mugezo had made to the community, especially on big events held by the ZANU-PF party. In 2005, the late President Mugabe visited Uzumba and donated computers at several schools in this community. *Babamunini* Mugezo presided over as master of ceremonies, a role he was selected for by people in his community. He had also been serving his community as an elections officer since 2005 because he was nominated by the district office. He said,

> Around 2005 the late former president Robert Mugabe visited schools in Mashonaland East donating computers, and our school is one of those he visited. During this visit I was appointed director of ceremony. Therefore, knowing that I could speak on such big platforms/occasions it made me an ideal candidate for voter education. At this point I was handpicked to be a voter educator because ZEC was decentralised according to provinces and each province would recruit from each district representatives to act as voter education officers. To get appointed the provincial office often looked for people who could address the public and had good public speaking skills, which is how I was picked. All functions that had happened at my school, for instance prize giving or annual general meeting I always served as the director of ceremonies.

In the 2005 elections he presided over a polling station that was about 150 km from his home. It is from this time he feels the rumours that were created about his association with the MDC intensified, especially because people did not understand his new role. The community had been advised not to listen to his information on elections and electoral processes. A colleague he was working with informed him that at one of the rallies held before the 2005 election the community he was supervising was informed to be on high alert because he was considered an agent working for the opposition. He dismissed the rumours because they were speculations that did not hold water.

When *babamunini* Mugezo was appointed as a voter educator in 2005 under ZEC, this electoral commission had just been established to replace the Electoral Supervisory Commission (ESC), which was run and controlled by the government since 1980 (Zimbabwe Electoral Commission 2019). It was created to stand as an independent body in accordance with recommendations of the SADC Principles and Guidelines Governing Democratic Elections (Zimbabwe Electoral Commission 2019). Thus, the political space at this point was increasingly being pushed towards electoral transparency, yet elections had been an avenue manipulated by the ruling party to remain in office. It is likely then that working in this space put some on the crossfire when their actions were considered a threat to the hegemony of ZANU-PF. The ruling party had often used the voter education sessions to intimidate, coerce and instil fear in the electorate (Sachikonye 2011; *Human Rights Watch* 2008). Yet as a voter educator, *babamunini* Mugezo was mandated by ZEC to inform the public (including door-to-door) about voting and elections, their rights, why it is important to register, when to register, how to register and why they should vote.

He described that,

> As voter educators we worked in teams of 12-13 people going around the district and visiting Voter Registration Centres. We would target the catchment area of the centre and visit communities around and interact with the people. We would hand out leaflets with details about voter registration, but before handing it out we would address the people and explain the contents of the pamphlet. We distributed posters as well. The material we distributed was made by ZEC and hence it was property of the government.

The above narration was shared to illustrate that in 2005 his duties came from a body appointed by the government. In mid-2007, there was another voter registration conducted in preparation for the 2008 harmonised election. He was appointed again to serve as a voter educator and worked closely with the Registrar's office which rolled out a programme to assist people without documentation to acquire birth certificates and identity document (ID) in preparation for the election registration. At this point he was made supervisor of a polling station in his area.

After discussing all the above roles, he had played to Muchandiona (the military commander) to dispel the allegations levelled against him, he was requested to provide supporting evidence. He collected a testimonial from the district office and submitted to the commander's base and was assured that he had been cleared of all suspicions. Since he had spoken to the base leaders, knowing that they oversaw planning the attacks, he says 'it never occurred to me that I would still be a target, because these are my people and as related persons there was a level of trust and respect I had for them which I thought would be reciprocated'.

The thought of running away was not a solution for *babamunini* Mugezo as he said,

> I had this thing on my mind that Uzumba is my birthplace and I had every right to be there, it's the place I belonged and ever really knew. If I were to run away because of the rumours being made about me and the opposition, what would become of me and where would I go to? Go to Harare? What for? I was working in Uzumba and my whole life revolved around my community. I knew I had never been involved in politics, well if I had been a member of the opposition then I would have had grounds to run away for my life, but I was not. In fact, running away would have confirmed their suspicions and how would I be able to come back? I used to think a lot about these things, and I knew I may be a target, but I was certain that running away was not going to resolve anything. So, I stayed, and since I was not an active member, I knew that my vote remained my secret.

Keeping his vote, a secret is one of the key messages that was related by the pamphlets he distributed for ZEC prior to the March 2008 elections. There was a sense of hope in him that those plotting to attack him would come around, especially because they knew each other, and he had done all they asked him to clear his name. However, the assurances were short-lived, and the rumours became a reality.

Facing the Ordeal

About two weeks prior to his attack two homes in his community belonging to MDC members were burned. In one of the homes an infant died, it was burnt to death. The other home belonged to a teacher and the roof of the house was damaged. Days before his attack there were about three people who were killed in his area. One of them was his aunt, *vatete* Rutendo from the paternal side, she used to live in Harare and her husband owned a business in Mutoko, they were well-off people. Anyone with links to Harare was treated with suspicion of being an opposition sympathiser and having a polluted ideology. She had a house in Harare where her children had remained staying and working, but occasionally she would visit them in the city, and they would also come home.

During our third interview, he narrated that a group of ZANU-PF youths raided his home in Uzumba on 21 May 2008 and accused him of being a 'sell-out'. This was during the period when the announcement of the presidential results had been delayed by over a month and ZEC was instead preparing for a run-off election (Magaisa 2016). In the first round of the 2008 elections held on the 29th of March, the electoral results of the parliamentary elections were released immediately after, but the presidential result was released on the 2nd of May, over a month after the polls had closed. These results were released amid reports of fraud and electoral rigging which made the opposition MDC to reject the pronouncements. The MDC had won the presidential election with 47.3%, followed by ZANU-PF with 43.2% but both parties had not secured a majority, creating the need for a re-run (Magaisa 2016).

The assailants who attacked *babamunini* Mugezo in May 2008, about twenty young men, were part of the military operative established by ZANU-PF to discipline those suspected of aiding the MDC to lead in the first round of elections. For the second round, ZANU-PF was canning the electorate to ensure victory. When the group approached *babamunini* Mugezo, they coerced him out of his home and took him to a bush that was fifty metres away. While in the bush he was asked to lie on the ground, face down, and they whipped him on the buttocks. He surrendered to the demands of his assailants and chose to stay calm by counting the strokes, but eventually lost count after 70 lashes.

They continued beating him non-stop, only posing a moment as they exchanged the whip. I asked him whether he knew the assailants and he mentioned that he could not see their faces, but his maid had managed to recognise one of them, who had remained in the house as the other group members exchanged beating him up. The guy who remained in the house ransacked it, looking for any material that could link him to the opposition, but did not find any. He ended up taking one of his phones which was on the charger.

He shared that, 'I never cried during the whole ordeal, the only thing I did was to tell them that what you want is a vote, but you are beating the vote?' At some point his assailants thought he was drunk because he had remained calm and never cried or made any noise. Earlier in the day, he had only had one beer but that would not have been enough to make him drunk. To explain his calmness, he stated that 'sometimes one has to resign to their fate', and in his case he surrendered because he had seen what they did to others accused of supporting the opposition in his community. He believes that the attackers did not mean to kill him because they only targeted his buttocks and not his head, which was a common modus operandi for killing their targets. When the beatings started it was around 12 midnight and very quiet, any sound of activities happening outside could travel a great distance. But, no one in the surrounding homes came to his rescue, even though they heard the attack (his ordeal captures the phenomena of *mhirizhonga* and *zhowe zhowe* examined in the previous chapter). His young children witnessed the ordeal while peeping through the window and could hear the beatings and chants of the assailants who were 'punishing' their father for supporting the opposition.

After nearly two hours of torture, he started feeling thirsty and asked the assailants for water. By this time, the other guy who had ransacked his house and was the leader of the group had joined them and informed his colleagues that the maid had identified him. He ordered the group to stop the beatings and commanded *babamunini* Mugezo to get up and run back to his home. This lucky escape he credits it to the Supreme Being, who acted through the maid that managed to identify one of the attackers, creating fear in them. He believes that should he have died from the attack; his family could have evoked the spirit of the ancestors to deal with the wrongdoers. In the Zimbabwean African setting, ancestors are spirit beings consisting of the departed family members of the living beings. The ancestral community (living dead) serves as a protector and guardian of the 'living living' (the people in the physical realm) and intercedes for the people to God, who is the creator of all beings, be it in the physical or metaphysical realm (Gelfand 1973; Nyathi 2015). These spirit beings can punish those who cause harm on others, as will be discussed later in this chapter and Chapter 4.

When the ringleader stopped the beatings, he advised him not to drink water immediately as that would affect him because his blood flow had been disrupted by the beatings. He got up slowly and dragged his bruised body back into the house. Once in his home he checked on his children and noticed they were all fine, then went to bed. He found his remaining mobile phone that was hidden under the pillow and contacted some relatives and his wife to inform them about the attack. He passed out and woke up around 6 a.m., then arranged his trip to Harare to seek refuge.

When he made it to Harare, he was assisted by a relative to locate services of a civil society organisation (CSO) that was attending to victims of political violence. During this period, some civil society actors risked their lives by facilitating the provision of medical, legal, psychological and social support to victims and survivors of violence. In the case of *babamunini* Mugezo, a Harare-based CSO[3] recorded an account of his attack and facilitated his admission to a private hospital where they paid all the medical bills. Within ten days of admission his health deteriorated to a life-threatening state because he could not pass waste and the whole body was swollen. The medical team attending to him solicited advice from a kidney specialist who ran tests and concluded that he had suffered a kidney failure. The specialist recommended a dialysis treatment but advised him that three outcomes were likely to occur: (i) the treatment could be successful and his body would return to a healthy state, (ii) the treatment could flush out everything but he may need to stay on dialysis for the rest of his life, and (iii) given that he was already weak his body might not cope, which could result to death.

His spouse gave consent for the doctors to go through with dialysis and his treatment involved two sessions a week over a period of three weeks. Each session took about five hours and after the sixth session his kidneys were working efficiently, enabling him to start other medical procedures to treat his bodily wounds. While still in hospital, he recalls seeing many patients who were victims of violence. Several of his hospital mates had come from different places, for example Buhera, Harare, Chitungwiza, Makoni, Mount Darwin, Mudzi and Uzumba, but their wounds were similar, indicating that the attacks were systematic and well-choreographed. Patients admitted in the same ward with *babamunini* Mugezo had open wounds on their back, buttocks, legs and head, which indicated that they had been beaten using a sharp object or rod that cut deep into the flesh. These effects were also noted in the 2008 Human Rights Watch report '*Bullets for Each of You*'. Some of the patients were only hospitalised several days after the attack and their wounds had developed gangrene. In his case, he was admitted early and doctors diagnosed that he had incurred extensive haematomas of his buttocks, thighs and haematuria. Apart from the dialysis, he required debridement and skin grafts for the haematomas. He spent nearly two months in hospital and by the time he was discharged the run-off election had occurred.

After his discharge, he only went back to his workplace in Uzumba to submit a letter of transfer and moved his family to Harare. He worked in Harare for a few months and went into exile in a country in Asia, but his family has not been able to join him. On the day he moved from *kumusha* to Harare he met Mairasa, his former schoolmate and local council chair at the shopping centre. He approached him and the other party he was talking to (a youth member in ZANU-PF) and greeted them. They responded to him but quickly dispersed making the remark that they were rushing for an appointment. He commented that coming face to face with Mairasa made him realise that he was ashamed because he avoided contact.

In their socio-cultural practice when familiar people meet, they shake hands and exchange greetings. But when he approached Mairasa the parties avoided making contact, which he interpreted as *kunyara* (shying away). Given that Mairasa had been boastful at rallies held after the attacks on *babamunini* Mugezo, it was difficult for the parties to meet face to face. *Babamunini* Mugezo had a habit of *kubudira vanhu pachena* (being frank or coming out in the open), and he indicated that when he approached Mairasa, it was his way of demonstrating that he was not afraid of him.

Living in Exile

In March 2009 *babamunini* Mugezo migrated for work in the Asia region. He indicated that his decision to move was based on two reasons: first, a sense of fear that he may be hunted down and attacked since he knew those who orchestrated his attacks; second, economic hardships because living in Harare was increasingly becoming expensive. He acquired new expenses in relation to housing costs, transport fees and the food shortages in Zimbabwe at the time were making the cost of living unbearable. A relative that was already living abroad linked him with an Australian recruiting agent that helped him secure a teaching post in the Asia region. Thus, human and economic insecurities drove his move to a new location in the hope of securing a better future for his family.

Even though he now lives abroad, he remains in a state of despair because he is separated from his family. He stated,

> The challenge of living in the diaspora is that sometime the nature of work you do doesn't give much to bring your family and the environment here is not the same as home. Our culture is different and the language issue as well, I would not want to uproot my family. It is better to continue working and send the money home.

Adjusting to a new environment was a difficult process for him because there are fewer Zimbabweans and African people in the country he is working. Unlike people who migrated to neighbouring countries such as South Africa, Zambia, Mozambique and Botswana, for the first three years of his stay, he was the only black person in his neighbourhood. It took him almost a year to make friends with two other Africans (one from Ghana another from Seychelles) he eventually met because they lived about 12 km from his area. These discussions we had about his experiences of living abroad brought to the fore questions of indigeneity, race and belonging. There is a Shona proverb that captures his predicament, *mwana washe muranda kumwe* which means a person of royalty may be treated as a slave in a foreign land. This occurs because your royal privileges and humanity may not necessarily be valued by those who consider you foreign. Hence, the expression holds that one's privileges can only be ascertained within the kinship, the further away one moves from their roots (where the umbilical cord that holds their lineage lies), the less valued they become.

Arguably, his sense of belonging and birth rights have waned off because he is in foreign territory. He added,

> If someone moves to South Africa it is easier to blend because we have a bit of things we share. Also, if one moves to the UK, you will find several Zimbabweans and can eventually build friendships among people who understand you and your culture because you come from the same country. But where I am, when I first arrived, I was the only black person in the neighbourhood. I got to know about two other Africans who were staying at least 12km away from here, one was a woman from Seychelles married to a native, the other was a guy from Ghana, but the rest of the people were natives or foreigners but from within the region or Caucasian. There is a difference in treatment, if you are a black person and Caucasian.

The above narrative captures the state of precariousness and perpetual isolation witnessed by some black persons because of the politics of race in the Asian region. What seems to determine this sense of foreignness in his new location is his skin colour. He added,

> The economy here is difficult for a black African without a university qualification to get employed. They do not recognise my teaching diploma. So, my Media Studies degree has become useful in acquiring a work permit and securing a job. But my spouse only has a diploma and will not be able to get a teaching job here or a work permit because they expect you to have at least a degree if you are black. They do not seem to have the same requirements for white people, for example I recently worked with a young white guy from South Africa he did not have a university degree, he registered to study with UNISA when he was already here working. It happens a lot that white people are assumed to be naturally knowledgeable and do not need to prove their skills unlike black people. You also find that the locals here *vane kakukuza varungu kavainako asi isu vanhu vatema vanoti tarisira pasi* (they have high praises for white people but look down upon black people).

It has been difficult for him to bring his family because of stringent immigration policies used to control movement of persons of colour from Africa in comparison with white persons. These disparities add to his consciousness of difference as he raised challenges of being black and African (here referring to skin colour and place of origin) in a territory that devalues people of colour. Despite learning the local language, he still feels foreign because of the race relations embedded in his new territory. What continues to fuel these notions of difference is coloniality of being. This form of coloniality is observed in the classification of human beings using ideas of race that put some people as superior beings to others (Maldonado-Torres 2007). Through colonialism, colonial powers have forged ideas of a European race that is peculiar and superior to non-white population groups, which still exists in the global arena. These race categories have stratified the society through noxious values of difference that present blackness and the African as inferior and subhuman (Mazrui 2005; Mudimbe 1994). In this hierarchy of race that exists in his new environment what he observes is an order of superiority that places a white person at the top, Asian in the middle and the black African at the bottom.

These continued sufferings and disparities are not necessarily addressed by mainstream writings on transitional justice because they attend to violence in a linear temporality and within a limited locality. The struggles he has encountered may seem to follow a chronological timeframe, but his experiences have been influenced by multiple temporalities and realities, which he feels would not be addressed by the current government initiatives of justice. His only hope of returning to Zimbabwe is when the government seizes to oppress the masses, suggesting that transitional justice needs to dismantle the power imbalances within the existing political landscape.

Addressing the Violence

When *babamunini* Mugezo was attacked, there were two other close relatives involved in planning the attack. One of them was *babamudiki* Mudhinda—an uncle and younger brother to his father—and the other was *munin'ina wake* Reason, a cousin and son to the uncle. *Babamudiki* Mudhinda is a stepbrother to vaChibundwa, the father of *babamunini* Mugezo, the two brothers were born by the same mother. This means that *babamunini* Mugezo's paternal grandmother is the blood link between his father and uncle. Two other community members who were attacked during this period were close relatives to *babamunini* Mugezo through the same paternal grandmother link. There is *vatete* Rutendo, mentioned earlier who was murdered and vaChadoka, who was beaten and had to relocate to another district. *Vatete* Rutendo was a cousin to both *babamudiki* Mudhinda and vaChibundwa, their mothers (i.e. grandmothers to *babamunini* Mugezo) were blood sisters, making her *hanzvadzi* (sister) to the two. On the contrary, vaChadoka and *babamudiki* Mudhinda were related through inter-clan marriages because Reason's elder brother had married the sister of vaChadoka, which made the three parties *vakurungai* (in-laws).

Weeks before the attacks a military operation commanded by Muchandiona (mentioned earlier) had set up a base/camp in their community from where the attacks were organised. Youths in the community were recruited and indoctrinated to terrorise targeted subjects. The operation commander, Muchandiona, a local community member, had a younger brother who was active in the MDC structures but reports have it that when the run off campaigns started he ordered his brother to make an apology at a ZANU-PF rally which got him off the hook (he was pardoned). This same commander was often seen visiting *babamudiki* Mudhinda's homestead because he was a friend to Reason. Both Reason and Muchandiona had served in the Zimbabwe Defence Forces (ZDF), though Reason retired from service early. Reason was a leader in the ZANU-PF youth league structures for Uzumba and the two are said to have collaborated in planning the attacks. More so, his father *babamudiki* Mudhinda was in the ZANU-PF structures and had been elected to office. *Babamunini* Mugezo stated,

> Chadoka's sister was married to Reason's brother which made the two in-laws. However, Chadoka was attacked and both Reason and *babamudiki* Mudhinda were in the know but did nothing to stop it. There is also *vatete* Aunty Rutendo who was murdered. *Babamudiki* Mudhinda was a

> brother to my aunt because their mothers were blood sisters. I can safely say *babamudiki* Mudhinda was involved in planning the attacks because *vanhu vakatirakasha* (the people who attacked us) were sometimes having meetings in his compound with his son and from there they monitored our movements.

He added that,

> *Vatete* Rutendo was also married *kwa*Nhembe (to the Nhembe's) and her brother in-law's wife, Tseurai, is an active member of ZANU-PF, *aishanda nana* Reason (she worked with Reason, her brother-in-law). Let's say *babamudiki* Mudhinda had a grudge against his sister, aunty Rutendo, but why did the sister-in-law [referring Tseurai] also cooperate in the plot instead of warning her in-law to flee.

VaChadoka mentioned above was a teacher and colleague to *babamudiki* Mugezo. He lived less than 100 m from the homestead of *babamudiki* Mudhinda, which made them close neighbours. When vaChadoka was attacked both Reason and *babamudiki* Mudhinda were aware but did not prevent the incident, an omission that was interpreted by family members as betrayal of trust and co-values that bind *ukama* (family ties). Similarly, they were aware of the planned attacks on their aunt, *vatete* Rutendo. *Vatete* Rutendo was married to the Nhembe's and her brother-in-law's wife called Tseurai was active in ZANU-PF structures in the same area. *Maiguru* Tseurai was reported to have had several interactions with *babamudiki* Mudhinda, Reason and Muchandiona. This suggests that she was knowledgeable of the planned violent activities that happened after the March 2008 elections.

Descriptions of the family ties between the parties that were directly wounded and those who were involved in plotting the attacks indicate a sense of betrayal and deepening of rifts at the interpersonal level. Their attacks were days apart and caught the attention of *mhuri yese* (the whole family—immediate and extended). Despite *babamudiki* Mudhinda, Reason and *maiguru* Tseurai not being the ones who physically attacked *babamunini* Mugezo, vaChadoka and *vatete* Rutendo, their cooperation and involvement with the party that organised the attacks rendered them responsible at the family level. *Paukama hwemhuri* (in accordance with family ties) in the life world of the studied communities, *hama nehama* (related persons) should defend each other, maintain respect for life, dignity, humility and *kudanana* (compassionate love). Upholding these values is crucial to keeping social harmony and prosperity in the *mhuri* (family), which consists of the living beings, living dead and future unborn. It is also an exercise of *hunhu hwakanaka*, the good traits that form the ethical code that binds people together, by giving guarantees of holding life as a shared enterprise.

When *babamunini* Mugezo was still in hospital, he was visited by *vana sekuru* (the uncles' who are brothers to his paternal grandmother) and they showed concern over the ordeal he had faced. He shared that,

> My uncles, brothers to my paternal grandmother, visited me when I was still in hospital and showed a lot of remorse over my ordeal. They were deeply saddened. I gave them my condolences for the death of aunty [aunty Rutendo was buried when he was still in hospital] and they informed me that they no longer considered Mudhinda a part of the family [they ostracised him].

Babamunini Mugezo indicated that tempers were high during the funeral of his aunt, with some family members charging and threatening to revenge with physical attacks. To resolve the matter and retain harmony in the family, *vana sekuru vakaita dare* and agreed *kuramwa* babamudiki Mudhinda (they held a family caucus and resolved to ostracise his uncle Mudhinda). *Dare* as mentioned by babamunini Mugezo is the Shona translation of the term court. This court falls under the 'customary' or 'tradition based' justice systems exercised by the studied communities. It is an assembly where people gather to deliberate issues.

Where the terms 'tradition-based' and 'customary' as mentioned above are interchangeably used in this book, I will be referring to justice processes that are rooted in the socio-cultural and historical practices of the specific community (Huyse and Salter 2008). These practices form part of the broader indigenous African legal customs and are associated with hearings, rituals and ceremonies inherent in value systems of African communities (Benyera 2014). Custom is however a contested term that carries varying socio-cultural and legal connotations to various settings.

Some scholars have described custom as the socio-cultural habits of a grouping that are regular, habitual or convergent (Hart 1994; Himonga 2011). In some instances, customs have legal standing because they exert a sense of obligation that enforces pressure to conform on the part of those to whom the obligation applies (Himonga et al. 2014). For example, among some in the studied communities, it is considered good behaviour to greet your elders or assist them when carrying weighty goods. These social behaviours are good mannerisms, one would not necessarily be sanctioned to court for failing to act in this manner.

On the contrary, *kuurayisa or kuuraya* (murder) as happened to aunty Rutendo, or the beatings that occurred to babamunini Mugezo and vaChadoka are forbidden behaviours that can be sanctioned through the *dare*. What informs a sense of restraint around these acts is the recognition by those bound by the norms and values of the constituent group—i.e. self-restraint, defending each other, maintaining respect for life, dignity, humility and *kudanana* (compassionate love)—which makes these principles their living customary law.

Diala (2017: 154) defines living customary law as customs of the people, developed through adaptation to transitions that occur to their communities, be it political, socio-economical, ecological or spiritual. Living customary law carries legal weight through the moral sanctions it renders among the practising group, which is why when one's behaviour contravenes the held principles, they are sanctioned by their constituent social grouping. The living customary law covered in this book draws from the norms and values (*tsika nemagariro*) of the studied communities which are underpinned by *hunhu. Hunhuism* dictates that *munhu ane hunhu* (a cultured person) is endowed by a disposition to act virtuously, which is why the actions of *babamudiki* Mudhinda, Reason and *maiguru* Tseurai were considered to have contravened the shared values of their family grouping. Their co-values include *kugarisana nevamwe* (living in harmony), *kuzvininipisa* (being humble), *kudyidzana* (friendship or fellowship), *kuzvibata* (self-discipline), *rukudzo* (respect), *kushanda nesimba* (industrious), and *kudzoreka* (teachable spirit), as examined in the previous chapter. The family elders held a *dare* to deliberate on the actions of the accused parties and resolved to ostracise them. At a family *dare* the goal is to *kuraira* (giving counsel), *kutsiura* (instilling discipline/reprimanding), *kudzoredzanisa* (reconciling) and in extreme cases *kuranga* (rendering punishment) such as the ostracising.

In the studied communities a *dare* gathering can be conducted under the guidance of family elders, community leaders or traditional authorities who have moral authority to mediate or adjudicate on a matter. These actors make up the three-tier of the customary justice system, which consists of a family court, village court and the chief's court. A family *dare* occurs at household level and is presided over by family elders, such as the caucus held by *babamunini* Mugezo's uncles discussed above. The village court and chief's courts are conducted by a village head, head person or chief who are community leaders in rural areas. A village head, head person and chief in ascending order make up the leadership structure at the community level, and often reside within reach of the community members. The village and chief's courts are recognised by the government of Zimbabwe through the Traditional Leaders Act (Chapter 29: 17) and Customary law and Local Courts Act (Chapter 7: 5).

The *dare* justice system, however, has limited jurisdiction because it only applies to matters enforceable under customary laws, and these are cases of a civil nature (Constitution of Zimbabwe 2013). Several community members and traditional authorities that I engaged with during the study maintained that they often intervene in issues beyond their statutory jurisdiction. This happens in cases that affect the social harmony of the community, which includes dealing with *kuponda* or *kuurayisa munhu* (acts of murder) and *kurovana zvinodeura ropa* (fights that involve spilling of blood) because it evokes bad omen in their land. Several studies have shown that anywhere between 70 and 90% of justice needs on the African continent, and globally, are met outside of the state-led justice system (Chirayath et al. 2005). This is certainly the case with the studied communities because their priority is to repair relational harms and restore harmony, which is best offered by their tradition-based justice system. A *dare* is a highly regarded platform for engagement among local communities because they regularly use it to deliberate and resolve any issues or points of concern. It is a platform they rely on for justice because of the moral values attached to the principles of *hunhu* they share.

Symbolism and Significance of Ostracising Family Members Implicated in Violence

When the family *dare* resolved to excommunicate *babamudiki* Mudhinda, it was an act of justice that was sanctioned from their shared values. Their justice involves *kutsiura* (chastising), *kuraira* (giving counsel), *kuranga* (instilling discipline) and *kudzoredzanisa* (reconciling). Hence, *kuramwa nana sekuru* (being ostracised by the uncles) was an extreme measure of *kuranga* (disciplining) in that it is tantamount to being cursed.

In accordance with their Shona customs, a maternal uncle is considered *amai* (mother figure) because they are a sibling to the mother or grandmother and can play the role of a mother as I indicated in Chapter 2 under the phenomenon *matengana gudo*. One's position within the family is not fixed, but rather assigned depending on the performative role they are expected to partake within the family unit. This organising might seem only applicable to nuclear family settings, but in the realities of the communities studied *munhu wese ihama* (everyone is family). Emphasis is placed on interconnective ties that exists among people because everyone is born into a family, whether it is single headed or nuclear.

It is their cultural belief that when you have been ostracised you become exposed to a lot of misfortune. For example, losing a job or falling ill and failing to get a medical diagnosis. In their socio-cultural understanding nothing happens without a cause, both the good and bad in life have a spiritual force that drives it. When such misfortunes occur, they tend to turn to spiritual and religious figures for solutions for example consulting *n'anga* or *maporofita* (traditional healers or prophets). These figures could advise that there is a bad omen that needs to be rebuked, but this process usually requires some family members to assist. If one has been disowned it becomes difficult to get support from the family, especially where some issues require a mother figure. *Babamunini* Mugezo shared that,

> *Mumhuri pane macultural* (in the family there are cultural) ceremonies and rituals where the mother figure plays a crucial role, for example

> burial, unveiling of a tombstone, lobola, *kuperekwa* and *masungiro*. When such events occur, there is an expectation that the mother figure will be present to perform the rites of a mother which ensures the event is successful.

A mother is considered the lifeline of a clan or family in the sense that she brings forth life in beings through birth, but before one is birthed they are carried in the womb of a woman, which is the incubator that gives them life throughout the gestation period. There is a special spiritual bond between the living, and the dead embodied by the spirit of a mother, in that the mother figure is bestowed with blessings which they usher to their offspring. When one is ostracised by a mother figure symbolically the ancestral family disowns the individual. Once this family bond has been severed one could lose blessings and protection from the cosmological community hence, they hold to the belief that *kusina amai hakuendwe* (meaning life is difficult without a mother). Moreover, the ancestors would be angered, and this tends to evoke avenging spirits called *kutanda botso* (facing the wrath of bad actions) that creates vicious cycles of pain and misfortune examined in the next section.

Was This Justice?

I was intrigued by the explanations that *babamunini* Mugezo gave around the recourse his family took to deal with the relational harms that occurred in the 2008 electoral violence. It became clear to me that justice had been administered at the family level to repair the interpersonal relations. However, I remained uncertain as to whether the resolution taken at the family caucus met the justice needs of *babamunini* Mugezo as a person who experienced direct violence. I therefore asked him the question: How about at a personal level, could you say justice was served? To which he replied,

> Yes, I think so because in whatever circumstance as siblings or relatives in our culture we are there to help each other in times of need, sorrow

> or happiness. When there are challenges, we ought to work together and cover each other's back. So, if you are found partaking in activities with the enemy then you are the enemy to the family. The family can discard you as punishment but also to distance themselves from the bad character you have become, especially when you have shown to be someone *asingadzoreke* (unreproachable person). They will be accusing you of failing to be responsible enough to protect your own. So, it is as good as *wakakonzera rufu rwacho iwewe* (you caused the death). *Kana vanasekuru vakuramwa* (when the uncles deject you) there is justice in the sense that you are an enemy and we cannot continue liaising with the enemy. Also, they surrender you to the universe for your judgement. They will leave you *wave negumbo rimwe* (standing on one foot), and you are no longer complete *wave chirema* (you are disabled).

In the above response he expressed that when a person absconds from their family obligations, they become an enemy to the co-group. The ruling made by the family elders was enough because they evoked the universe to deal with the accused, and often this process leaves one in a state of obscurity. They consider this *kuva mujere rako wega* (being imprisoned by your own conscience), the severest of punishment that a human being can be exposed to. This act of isolation and being left to your own conscience is an overt form of punishment that pushes one to re-evaluate their being, especially because they believe that *upenyu vanhu* (life is a shared enterprise). He added that,

> I am satisfied with the decision *yana sekuru* (made by the uncles). As an individual *ndinogona kutanga ndiine* (I may start off with) resentment especially because of the wounds inflicted on my body, but with time they heal. In the early days I was very bitter, now my pain has faded. When the wounds heal you notice that life still needs to be lived and you tell yourself that this person is no longer a part of our lives [indicating that the personal is linked to the interpersonal]. You also notice that the one who hurt you their life has not been moving smoothly or as good as your own. Yet, when they were participating in violence, they had expectations of benefitting from political office. Many of those material rewards did not materialise, because *kune vamwe vaive nekugun'una pamusoro pako* (people had bitterness or made utterances to the universe about your bad actions).

Babamunini Mugezo shared that the 2008 experiences have brought three life lessons to his community which I discuss below.

Lesson 1: When you don't have a space of belonging your life is meaningless and that torture is more severe on anyone.

Six years after the 2008 violence his uncle, *babamudiki* Mudhinda, was expelled and evicted from the ZANU-PF party and political office. This happened during the ousting of the former Vice-President Joyce Mujuru who was sacked in December 2014 on allegations of plotting to kill and remove President Mugabe (Hungwe 2014). The expulsion of his uncle was interpreted by some in his family as the comeback of karma. He stated,

> *Vakadzingwa mubato*, meaning he was also rejected by his party and became a victim. *Vangovawo tsuro, havasisina masimba nechiremerera chavaive nacho. Vave munhu akapwa* (he is now a pauper and no longer has the authority and stature he had as a political figure. He now looks pale).

These drastic changes in social status demonstrated that tables had turned for the worst for his uncle. He added,

> If political violence is to happen again, he could be attacked. Take for instance the coup that happened in 2017, Mnangagwa had been pushed out by the G40[4] and went into exile. But he returned with the backing of the military and war veterans and removed Mugabe from office and some in the G40 had to flee into exile.

The vicious cycle of violence discussed above illustrates the issues of factionalism that has ravaged the political landscape of Zimbabwe. Both the ZANU-PF and MDC parties have witnessed divisionism that has resulted to intra-party conflicts, for example the attack on former MDC-T Vice-President Thokozani Khupe by MDC youths during the funeral of the party leader Morgan Tsvangirai (Dube 2018). It contributed to the split of the MDC-T after the death of the founding leader Tsvangirai. Within ZANU-PF intra-party violence was witnessed during the removal of President Mugabe in November 2017 and tensions still prevail within the party (Rogers 2019). A lot of uncertainty and thirst for power remains in the lives of political figures in Zimbabwe which arguably fuels divisionism, intolerance and violence.

From the perspective of the studied communities, those who orchestrate violence on others while in positions of leadership will reap what they sow (*vanorumwa nechokuchera*). President Mugabe's nephew Patrick Zhuwao while speaking to press about the death of his uncle claimed that the former president had died in exile in Singapore, which contested the government's stance that he was away obtaining medical treatment (SABC Digital News 2019a). The removal of Mugabe and some members of the G40 by the Lacoste faction in ZANU-PF led by Emmerson Mnangagwa (incumbent president) points to the effects of falling out of the Mugabeism system discussed by Ndlovu-Gatsheni (2015). Exiled members of the G40 such as Saviour Kasukuwere, Patrick Zhuwao and Jonathan Moyo are no longer protected by the system that enabled them to orchestrate violence on others. For instance, Jonathan Moyo was the brains behind the introduction of restrictive policies that featured post-2000 such as AIPAA and POSA, which have caused some citizens to be subjected to inhumane treatment by state security agents. In the early 2000s, Moyo was the Minister of Information and facilitated the roll out of propaganda machinery within the media and sociopolitical spaces that advanced populist narratives and patriotic history created by the ZANU-PF party (Ndlovu 2019).

Babamudiki Mudhinda was dejected by his own family and the political party that he had sacrificed his family for. Those who see his present state consider him to be *munhu ave pambene* (left in the bare) and lacking a place of belonging. *Babamunini* Mugezo stated,

> When we see this, we do not just look at is as political fights but believe the spirit of those they victimised has caused their suffering and dejection. From this view justice has been saved. *Iwewe hausisina kugadzikana wave kutambudzika* like the time *yataive tiri* (you are facing challenges just as we went through troubles). But in their case the problem is a double tragedy; (i) the system you benefitted from has rejected you (ii) the people you hurt have disowned you, nobody wants to associate with you. In the end *unenge wave mujere rako wega* (you are imprisoned by your own conscience). *Upenyu vanhu* (life is a shared enterprise) and when you

> don't have a space of belonging your life is meaningless and that torture is more severe on anyone.

A learning point for his community drawing on the predicament facing his uncle has been '*vanhu tinofanira kubata vamwe vanhu mune zvakanaka*' (we should treat all with dignity) irrespective of your stature in society. This relates to the principle of being humble and respectful enshrined in their co-values as a community. There are politicians in their community who still have honour and respect because they refrained some party members from using violence in elections. For these actions they carry no curse from *vadzimu venyika* (ancestors) and continue to associate with everyone well. The studied communities believe that the living and the dead do not refrain people from having differences in opinion, but their co-values require them to exercise self-restrain, discipline and respect always. Failure to uphold these values can result to dejection by both the living and the dead which they call '*nyika inokuramba*'.

Lesson 2: In a community that values seniority losing self-respect and stature in the family reduces the being to nothingness.

During the 2018 primary elections, his former schoolmate and council chair Mairasa lost his political seat to another party member. It was shared by participants that his constituency rejected him citing issues of cruelty and accusing him of not being progressive. This fall from political office symbolised that he had been rejected by the people.

The fallout happened at a time when Mugabe had been removed from office and those associated with him were being chopped off from the party structures. This is not to say only those associated with Mugabe lost seats in ZANU-PF. But the new leadership was working on the mantra Operation Restore Legacy[5] which in some instances resulted to exclusion of persons considered rogue elements. Life after the fall of the G40 has seen some elements who were deemed highly likely aligned with this faction or had been tainted in acts that gave a bad name to the party at the community level being side-lined in attempts to renew the face of the party. In the case of Mairasa his political career came to an end because people from his constituency linked him to the 2008 electoral violence and accused him of abusing state resources. Thus, *vanhu vakamuramba* (people dejected him) because of his past actions that were not atoned for. *Babamunini* Mugezo argued,

> When you fall from a party like ZANU-PF, it is hard to stand on your own. It's difficult to consider forming your own party, to run as an independent candidate or even join the opposition, you are doomed. It becomes difficult to remain relevant and your career crumbles. The benefits also dwindle, and you are no longer cushioned by the system that enabled you to terrorise others and plunder state resources. *Ave kutotambura sevamwe, munhu aimbova* ne access to inputs and development projects *dzaitungamirwa nehurumende* (he now struggles like everyone for someone who used to have access to inputs and development projects led by the government). As a political figure he would be the first to benefit or get special preference but now *angova tsuro* (he is a pauper). *Nekutambura uku munhu anodzimara adzoka ega kuzogadzirisana nevamwe nekuti munyama unenge wamusona* (These hardships force a person to comeback and resolve issues because misfortunes will be haunting).

The sense of being haunted by bad spells instils compulsion for justice to the studied communities because they believe in the power of the universe to deal with those who misbehave. Undergoing torture from within or spiritual tormenting causes havoc in one's life which they believe is effective in pushing people to return to their shared values. This is captured by the expression *munhu anodzimara adzoka ega kuzogadzirisana nevamwe* (a person ends up coming back to repair relations) because life is a shared enterprise one cannot thrive without the good wishes and support of their family. Moreover, by losing political office Mairasa lost his stature in the community because *vanhu vaigunun'una pamusoro pake* (people were bitter and begrudged). He was deserted by the party and lost his standing in the community. *Babamunini* Mugezo stated that,

> The moral lesson drawn from this experience is that when you are in position of authority do not abuse power nekuti *masimba vanhu* (authority comes from people). *Ukavabata zvakanaka uri mupolitics* (when you treat people well while in political office) they will treat you well *zvekuti even wabva mupower* (such that even when you leave office) people would still

> have respect for you. But *ukasafamba zvakanaka unoshaya chiremerera* (if your behaviour is questionable you will lose respect and honour).

The idea that power comes from people suggests that one's authority is rendered by the community and sanctioned by the same community. When one abuses their position of authority the community can withdraw respect and honour from you. In a setting that values seniority and honour losing self-respect means you have been reduced to nothing. To regain yourself and association with others one must atone to those who were wronged, hence justice is sanctioned by the spirits.

Lesson 3: The universe has its ways of retaining cosmic balance when it has been torn by violence.

There was also a former member of parliament (MP) and prominent businessman in Uzumba, Kundidana, who was involved in the violent operations that occurred in 2008. He is accused of sponsoring the violence materially by offering his business premises as a meeting point from which some ZANU-PF elements organised their attacks. In 2013, he lost in the primary election and since then his business operations have been dwindling. *Babamunini* Mugezo argued,

> Some could consider that he is facing economic hardships steaming from the collapse of the economy. But from a socio-cultural interpretation *munhu aive nema* retail shops *achifamba zvakanaka asi haachaita mushe* (someone who operated successful retail shops but now they are no longer performing well), you cannot rule out the works of a spell fighting him. There are still similar businesses at the centre that are thriving despite the economic turndown. He is now close to broke and failing to maintain operations, although he has not yet closed business, which would even be more dire. His family has also been facing challenges, lately his sons are reported to have fought with him in public.

In the socio-cultural context of the studied community, witnessing such *mhirizhonga* (i.e. father–son fights) means there are deep-seated spiritual battles facing the family. Even though Kundidana did not beat or murder people in 2008, the fact that he supported materially those who were involved could be causing the misfortunes he is incurring. *Babamunini* Mugezo added,

> People will be watching and v*anoita chigumbu newe* and *vanenge vachigunun'una* (they will be bitter and begrudging) which evokes bad spells on you. *Munhu haafanire kunge achinongedzwa nevanhu kunzi akaipa or ane mwoyo wakashata* (a person should not be pointed out as bad or evil hearted). This man like the council chairman, he lost authority, respect and honour in the community and is now a *punha* (a nobody). His dignity has been withdrawn.

The configuration that Kundidana is now a nobody demonstrates that he lost economic muscle and social respect. These changes have been necessitated by the bad spells evoked from people's discomfort with his conduct. *Kugunun'una* mentioned above is a form of relentless lamentations made by a person/s in a state of despair. This sense of restlessness of one's spirit at the hands of another disrupts cosmic harmony. Hence, utterances to the universe are considered prayers which bring forth relief by punishing those who have harmed others. In this case, the punishment has been a loss of political authority and economic hardships which they say '*zvinokudzikamisa*' (it humbles you). Thus, the justice they have witnessed is *kudzikamiswa* which in their view brings someone back to their senses and co-values shared by the community. A key lesson therefore is one should still treat everyone with dignity, love and humility regardless of their stature in society. These values bring back social harmony.

Conclusion

In the world sense of *babamunini* Mugezo the violence he witnessed destroyed the social bond of his family because those implicated in facilitating the attacks were his own blood. It is a taboo among his social grouping for one to partake in causing harm or the spilling of blood because it pollutes their cosmological community. Relational harms evoke *kugunun'una* which are lamentations and utterances to the universe that bring forth bad omen. Where people speak ill of your actions the universe responds to their burdened heart by cutting off spiritual benefits, especially when the mother figure rebukes the party by ostracising them.

Justice is an action that involves *kuraira* (giving counsel), *kuranga* (instilling discipline) and *kudzoredzanisa* (reconciling). It is an active process that brings one back to their senses and re-alignment with co-values of the community because *munhu vanhu* (You are Because, We Are). When one hurts others, they hurt themselves also, hence the need to always exercise *kuzvibata* (self-restain), *kugarisana nevamwe* (living in harmony), *kuzvininipisa* (being humble), *kudyidzana* (friendship or fellowship), *rukudzo* (respect) and *kudzoreka* (teachable spirit). Involving the spiritual realm to administer justice has been a central feature in the lives of the studied communities because *Mwari ndiye muzivi wazvose* (God is the harbinger of all things in life). Arguably, justice has been served because the afflicted parties are able to observe manifestations of bad omen on their assailants—*vari kurumwa nechekuchera* (reaping the seed of their violent actions)—which will cause them to return and repair relations to regain spiritual benefits. This return to repair relations forms their cycle of justice in that it is not only momentary, but a continuous process geared at renewing the essence of humanity. In the following chapter, I will unpack issues of spirituality, omen, fortune and remedies in greater detail.

Notes

1. Former President Robert Mugabe was forced to resign from office on 21 November 2017 after facing a military assisted deposal from office and expulsion from the ZANU-PF party. He was replaced by his former Vice-President Emmerson Mnangagwa whom he had expelled from the office and party on 7 November 2017 on accusations of 'disloyalty, disrespect, deceitfulness and unreliability' forcing him to flee into exile in South Africa (McKirdy 2017). Mnangagwa returned to the country after two weeks and took overpower through a military coup led by former army generals Sibusiso Moyo and Constantino Chiwenga, who is now in cabinet as Minister of Foreign Affairs and vice president, respectively (McKenzie et al. 2017).

2. When the MDC was formed in 1999 most of its members came from the unions since the leader Morgan Tsvangirai had been a secretary general of the ZCTU. It could be argued that being a chairperson of a housing cooperative that falls under the teachers' union made him to be suspected an agent of the MDC because of the associations that prevailed in this era between the opposition and unions.
3. The name of the organisation is not provided to protect the participant and the CSO that assisted him.
4. The G40 short for Generation 40, a rival faction within the ZANU-PF party that was led by Saviour Kasukuwere (former ZANU-PF national commissar and Minister for Local Government, Youth and Environment), Jonathan Moyo (former Minister of Higher and Tertiary Education), Patrick Zhuwao (former Minister of Public Service, Labour and Social Welfare) and Grace Mugabe the former first lady of Zimbabwe (Hodgkinson 2019). Members of this faction were expelled from the party when Mugabe was removed from office in November 2017.
5. Operation Restore Legacy is the code name for the military coup that began on 13 November 2017 leading to the forced resignation of former President Robert Mugabe on 21 November 2017. The allies to the president under the faction group G40 were also expelled from the ZANU-PF party leading some to seek refuge in exile (SABC Digital News 2019b).

References

Benyera, E. 2014. *Debating the Efficacy Transitional Justice Mechanisms: The Case of National Healing in Zimbabwe*. Doctoral Dissertation, University of South Africa, Pretoria.

Chinodya, S. 1990. *Harvest of Thorns*. Oxford, Oxon: Heinemann.

Chirayath, L., C. Sage, and M. Woolcock. 2005. Customary Law and Policy Reform: Engaging with the Plurality of Justice Systems. World Development Report Background Papers. Available from https://openknowledge.worldbank.org/handle/10986/9075. Accessed 26 September 2019.

Constitution of Zimbabwe. 2013. *Zimbabwe's Constitution of 2013*. Government Publications. Available from https://www.constituteproject.org/constitution/Zimbabwe2013.pdf. Accessed 14 April 2019.

Diala, A.C. 2017. The Concept of Living Customary Law: A Critique. *The Journal of Legal Pluralism and Unofficial Law* 49 (2): 143–165.

Dube G. 2018. *MDC-T VP Thokozani Khupe Beaten Up, Nearly Set on Fire in Hamlet at Tsvangirai Funeral*. Available from https://www.voazimbabwe.com/a/morgan-tsvangirai-thokozani-khupe-mdc-t-beaten-up/4262709.html. Accessed 17 October 2019.

Gelfand, M. 1973. *The Genuine Shona: Survival of Values of an African Culture*. Gwelo: Mambo Press.

Hart, H.L.A. 1994. *The Concept of Law*. Oxford: Oxford University Press.

Himonga, C., T. Nhlapo, I.P. Maithufi, M.S. Weeks, L. Mofokeng, and D. Ndima. 2014. *African Customary Law in South Africa: Post-Apartheid and Living Law Perspectives*. Cape Town: Oxford University Press Southern Africa.

Himonga, C.N. 2011. The Future of Living Customary Law in African Legal Systems in the Twenty-First Century and Beyond, with Special Reference to South Africa. In *The Future of Customary Law*, ed. J. Fenrich, P. Galizzi, and T. Higgins, 31–57. Cambridge: Cambridge University Press.

Hodgkinson, D. 2019. The Mnangagwa Era? Periodisation and Politics in Zimbabwe. *Journal of Southern African Studies* 45 (5): 981–992.

Human Rights Watch. 2008. "*Bullets for Each of You*": *State Sponsored Violence Since Zimbabwe's March 29 Elections*. Available from https://www.hrw.org/report/2008/06/09/bullets-each-you/state-sponsored-violence-zimbabwes-march-29-elections. Accessed 17 August 2019.

Hungwe, B. 2014. *Zimbabwe's Mugabe Sacks Vice President Joyce Mujuru Over 'Plot'*. Available from https://www.bbc.com/news/world-africa-30400178. Accessed 17 October 2019.

Huyse, L., and M. Salter (eds.). 2008. Traditional Justice and Reconciliation After Violent Conflict—Learning from African Experiences. Stockholm, International Institute for Democracy and Electoral Assistance (IDEA). Available from https://www.idea.int/publications/catalogue/traditional-justice-and-reconciliation-after-violent-conflict-learning. Accessed 22 November 2019.

Magaisa, A. 2016. *The Big Saturday Read: Remembering 27 June—Probably the Darkest Chapter in Zimbabwe's Electoral History*. Available from https://www.bigsr.co.uk/single-post/2016/07/02/The-Big-Saturday-Read-Remembering-27-June-%E2%88%92-probably-the-darkest-chapter-in-Zimbabwe%E2%80%99s-electoral-history. Accessed 29 October 2019.

Maldonado-Torres, N. 2007. On the Coloniality of Being. *Cultural Studies* 21 (2, 3): 240–270.

Mazrui, A. 2005. The Re-invention of Africa: Edward Said, V. Y. Mudimbe, and Beyond. *Research in African Literatures* 36 (3): 68–82.

McKenzie, D., S. Brent, and D. Angela. 2017. *Zimbabwe Is Under Military Control After Army Seizes Power from Mugabe*. Available from https://edition.cnn.com/2017/11/14/africa/zimbabwe-military-chief-treasonable-conduct/index.html. Accessed 28 November 2019.

McKirdy, E. 2017. *Robert Mugabe Fires Zimbabwe's VP, Paves Way for Wife to Succeed Him*. Available from https://edition.cnn.com/2017/11/07/africa/zimbabwe-mugabe-vice-president-mnangagwa/index.html. Accessed 28 November 2019.

Mudimbe, V.Y. 1994. *The Idea of Africa*. Oxford: James Currey.

Ndlovu, M. 2019. *'I Will Never Apologise for POSA and AIPPA' Says Jonathan Moyo*. Available from https://bulawayo24.com/index-id-news-sc-national-byo-154807.html. Accessed 27 March 2019.

Ndlovu-Gatsheni, S.J. (ed.). 2015. *Mugabeism? History, Politics, and Power in Zimbabwe*. New York: Palgrave Macmillan.

Nyamubaya, F. 1995. *Dusk of Dawn*. Harare: College Press.

Nyathi, P. 2015. *Ngozi: An African Reality…Ensuring Social Justice and Fairness*. Available from http://www.herald.co.zw/ngozi-an-african-reality-ensuring-social-justice-and-fairness/. Accessed 24 November 2019.

Orwell, G. 1946. *Animal Farm: A Fairy Story*. New York, USA: Harcourt, Brace and Company.

Rogers, D. 2019. *Two Weeks in November: The Astonishing Untold Story of the Operation That Toppled Robert Mugabe*. Johannesburg: Jonathan Ball Publishers.

SABC Digital News. 2019a. *In Conversation with Mugabe's Nephew, Patrick Zhuwao*. Available from https://www.youtube.com/watch?v=tBT9toYbZpM. Accessed 27 September 2019.

SABC Digital News. 2019b. *Reflecting on the Life of Mugabe: Saviour Kasukuwere*. Available from https://www.youtube.com/watch?v=jN3VHE9_1og. Accessed 27 September 2019.

Sachikonye, L. 2011. *When a State Turns on Its Citizens: 60 Years of Institutionalised Violence in Zimbabwe*. Oxford: African Books Collective.

Zimbabwe Electoral Commission. 2019. *Historical Background*. Available from https://www.zec.org.zw/pages/history. Accessed 2 December 2019.

4

Spirituality, Rituals and Remedy

Abstract Where official processes of transitional justice have not been successful, there remains a big need for rendering justice to affected parties. A focus on the local community is crucial because human loss, suffering and physical and metaphysical disruptions are experienced most by civilians and not government officials or their security agents. This chapter adopts the cosmological argument to bring forth ways in which participants in Buhera, Mudzi and Uzumba understand their realities and the relations they have with their environment. I argue that spirituality provides a holistic remedy to the harms incurred through rituals, ceremonies and reparations which restores harmony among cosmic beings. Whether it takes decades to resolve the matter, the studied communities believe in the effect of the spiritual realm in evoking justice.

Keywords Cosmological · Metaphysical · Cleansing · Ritual · Living being · Haunted · Avenging spirit · Compensation · Spirituality · Harmony · Ceremony

R. Murambadoro, *Transitional Justice in Africa*, Development, Justice and Citizenship, https://doi.org/10.1007/978-3-030-48092-9_4

Introduction

Spirituality informs the world sense of many people in the studied communities in terms of coming to terms with experiences of violence. Spirituality here refers to the belief in the powers of the universe, and this universe creates a network of relations among entities in the physical and metaphysical realms (Nigosian 1994: 4). In this chapter, I draw on the cosmological argument (Gale and Pruss 1999) to bring to the fore ways in which the studied communities understand their realities and the relations they have with their environment. Special attention will be given to lived experiences of four participants *mai* Mukwa, *babamunini* Mugezo, *ambuya* Meso and *babamukuru* Mutyairi to bring out the role of spirituality in addressing violence experienced in their communities. I argue that there is a cosmological sense to people's understanding of violence and justice, which cannot be understood without exploring how people relate within the cosmos. When violence occurs in the world sense of the research participants, it affects the network of relations of entities in the entire cosmological community consisting of living beings in relationship with each other, nature and spirit beings. To repair the damaged relationship between the cosmos-specific rituals, ceremonies and cleansing is required as discussed in this chapter.

Spiritism, Fortune and Omen

During the post-March 2008 elections, *mai* Mukwa lost her 20-year-old son Nherera who was murdered by ZANU-PF youth militias sanctioned by the party. Nherera was targeted while driving at Kotwa township in Mudzi. A group of assailants threw a petrol bomb on his car and opened fire, but he managed to escape from the vehicle together with his friend. The friend managed to run away but Nherera had been injured and could not run far, so he hid in a nearby bush. The group made a chase and abducted him then took him away to a bushy area in Nyamanyora a village in the area but closer to Mt Darwin (a neighbouring district). They opened fire and shot him at close range. He bled to death. The mother of deceased shared that,

> When my son did not return home on the day of the attack, my heart was not settled. I was troubled because I had heard news about the incident that happened at the township. The whole time he was absent I felt ill. I only believed the news of his death after viewing his body because I thought at least we have something to bury.

Even as I listened to the above story of how *mai* Mukwa's son was murdered, my heart was burdened and I had so many questions as to how she managed to pull it through. Those who attacked her son were fellow community members, people she had called neighbours and even relatives for a very long time. The death of Nherera was devastating on her because he was the eldest sibling taking care of the family since his father had died a few years earlier. In their custom when someone dies, they perform *nhamo*, which is a funeral ceremony that runs for a day or couple of days depending on the plans of the mourning family.

Her son's funeral was difficult for the family to arrange because of the political tensions that prevailed at the time. She stated,

> At his funeral people were not comfortable to come and mourn with us due to political tensions, the people who murdered my son were sanctioned by ZANU PF officials. His death had been well planned because they accused him of being an MDC member. As such, people were not free to attend his funeral because of fear of being attacked or labelled MDC supporters since my homestead had been tainted a residence of MDC members. Even church members could not assist with his funeral, my family had to follow our African customs.

In Chapter 2, I discussed the phenomenon *politics yapinda mumba* to illustrate how political feuds have damaged the ethos of the community relating to *kugarisana nevamwe* (living in harmony), *kuzvininipisa* (being humble), *kudyidzana* (friendship or fellowship), *kuzvibata* (self-discipline), *rukudzo* (respect) and *kubatirana* (working together) among others. The above narrative points to how political contestations became a hindrance for community members to partake in their collective moral duties in relation to funerals and dealing with a loss. *Rufu* is a crucial moment in the lives of studied communities because of the rites performed to the body and spirit of a deceased person. When one dies, *mutumbi* (the body) separates with *Mweya* (living spirit) and both have specific ways that they should be treated once one has died.

In this context, when a person dies people conduct *rufu* or *nhamo*, which is a ceremony of mourning, honouring and comforting the family of the deceased. *Shoko rerufu* (news about the passing of someone) is shared with v*anhu veukama* (relatives), *shamwari* (friends), *vavakidzani* (neighbours) and acquaintances who usually come forth to the residence of the deceased *kuzobata maoko* (paying last respect) and to comfort the bereaved family. They also give *mari yechema* which is a token to assist the bereaved with the funeral arrangements.

During *nhamo*, people gather to sing for the deceased and to give messages of comfort to the grieving family. There is, therefore, several entities within the family and community that perform different tasks that assist the bereaving family to go through with a funeral. Some *vanoimbira*, which are people who sing *dziyo dzekuchema mufi* (songs of mourning) and through music and dance they will be consoling the bereaved. Others preach or give messages of encouragement to the grieving; here, they can rely on religious texts such as the bible or proverbs. There are also people who go *kumapoto* and prepare meals for the parties attending the funeral.

The night before burial, *mutumbi wemufi* (the body of the deceased), is brought to the homestead they used to stay and lie in state. People perform an all-night service involving singing, dance and preaching. These performances are done *kureverera Mweya* (prayers to the universe wishing well for the spirit) of the deceased to find rest as the body is laid the following morning, and to strengthen the bereaved to come to terms with their loss.

Burial sites are mostly within the homestead, although in some villages they have a communal cemetery. In the case of Nherera, his body was laid to rest in his family compound among members of his clan which they call *kurara nevobwo*. A grave is usually dug by *hama dzemumusha* (community members) but the grave site marking, and initial digging is done by *hama yorudzi rwomufi* (a blood relative to the deceased). People are usually buried in the morning before midday or later in the afternoon. On the day of burial, *varoora vemumusha* (aunts who are wives to the mother's brother) are responsible for performing the last body wash on the deceased. During the body wash, close family members will be present *vachitaura nemutumbi wemushakabvu* (engaging with the corpse). This is done to prepare the body and spirit of the deceased for their new journey—the body returning to the soil and the spirit joining the forerunners of the clan. It must be noted that when one dies their life takes a new form as a living dead, and they remain an active member of the family; hence, much attention is given to the handling of one's remains.

Once the body has been bathed, the family conducts a final service and body viewing then they take the body for burial. When the body is being carried to the grave site, *varoora vemumusha* (sisters-in-law) are usually on the led spreading *mazambiya pasi* (spreading a wrap on the ground) for people carrying the coffin to walk over, which is a sign of paying respect to the deceased. At the grave site, a priest can say a prayer and recite biblical scripts as the body is laid to the ground. Close family members would also throw some soil on the coffin as they say their last words to their loved one. After burial people usually return to the main area of the compound and are washed hands as they come through and served a meal. These performances often help the bereaved to cope with their loss mainly because of the love and support they receive from family, friends and the greater community. It must be noted that the research participants considered both Christian practices and their cultural beliefs intertwined elements of their spirituality. They exercise religious pluralism in that though they follow Christianity—a Western-Judaic religion largely brought through colonialism—it has not necessarily replaced or erased their socio-cultural beliefs because African religions are dynamic and open to multi-culturalism (Gelfand 1981: 45). Instead, their African spiritualism absorbed Christianity and adapted it to their ways of being (Paris 1993); hence, they have remained connected with their cosmological community as observed in the rituals and ceremonies they perform such as *nhamo* explained above.

The political tensions that prevailed in 2008 made it difficult for some family members and the community to support *mai* Mukwa during her time of bereavement. She indicated that,

> A few people that came to pass their condolences had to be sneaky or come at night. In our living customs we are people who work together when one is facing difficulties, but I could not get any support because people were afraid of being caught in the crossfire because of the political tensions. In fact, I have been stigmatised because of my son's death over political matters.

The above narrative brings out ideas of community and collective action especially because they are settled along their clan lines and have communal values of working together. *Paukama* (among related persons) it is important to support each other in times of grief, troubles and happiness because it brings unity *mumhuri* (in the family). In times of difficulty, *Hunhu* requires people to have *kunzwirana* (empathy), *mushandirapamwe* (working together or collective efforts) and *kubatana* (togetherness or unity). Hence, they use the Shona proverb *chara chimwe hachitswanyi inda* meaning a single finger cannot squash a louse. This proverb indicates the importance of collective efforts in families and communities when faced with challenges. When people work together, the burden becomes lighter especially when dealing with a loss, but this could only be done by a few immediate relatives. The inhibiting of communal support during funerals of persons accused of being MDC agents was common post-2000; it occurred even with the deaths of Talent Mabika and Tichaona Chiminya the MDC activists mentioned in Chapter 2 of this book (Meldrum 2000). Isolating the grieving family deepened wounds because they were denied the opportunity to perform funeral rites for their loved one and to get psychosocial support.

Mai Mukwa's family had to rely on *kuviga pachivanhu* since church members could not attend, which meant that they had a small traditional burial. An elderly community member vaMbuswa explained that in their custom when someone is murdered, they perform a burial ritual that involves *mbanda* and traditional beer called *nhopi*. *Mbanda* is a cutting from an endogenous tree they consider sacred that is planted on the grave as they bury the deceased. This cutting has properties that protect the spirit of the dead from being suppressed by those who wronged the deceased, which they call *kutsipika*. It is believed that when one has died unceremoniously their spirit will be aggrieved and can come back to seek justice from those in the wrong. But in some instances, the wrongdoers may try to evade *kupfukirwa nemufi* (being wrestled by the spirit of the deceased) by using divination. Hence, *mbanda* and *nhopi* are key practices of keeping the spirit of the deceased alive to fight for justice. *Nhopi* is made in *chikari* (a form of clay pot) using millet, sacred herbs and water. One traditional leader in Mudzi chief Saimba explained that,

> The beer mixture is boiled and set aside to rest. On burial the *nhopi* is poured on the grave uttering a message to the Creator and all ancestors of the family that herewith another member of the family that has departed. You are aware of how the deceased passed, may you stand in and resolve the matter as well as prepare a path that allows him to return to us and be a contributing member to the family. When they are done, they break the clay pot by throwing it on the grave.

When these burial rites are performed, the spirit of the deceased begins a new journey in which it avenges those responsible. *Mai* Mukwa shared that,

> My son's spirit is not at rest we sometimes hear news that those who were responsible for his death they sometimes act insane, but they have not yet approached us to resolve the matter.

This indicates that the justice process for Nherera has begun because his spirit is tormenting those responsible for his death. For someone who cannot make sense of how this spiritual realm operates, it might seem like justice has not occurred. But it is important to observe that in the socio-cultural sense of the studied communities, justice is not a momentary event, rather a process that in some cases takes a whole journey of one's life and generations to come. When a person dies unnaturally (in this case murdered), their spirit does not find rest among the *vebwo* (kinship), where the body is laid. The spirit only finds rest when compensation has been offered by the person responsible or their family in consultation with the relatives of the deceased. This process is very complex because the form of compensation required might be too steep for the accused to clear up; hence, the easiest way is *kudzinga mweya* or *kusairira kune vamwe* (fanning the avenging spirit) or *kutsipika* as stated earlier, but the problem will persist and affect many more people.

Spiritual agency is therefore central to their justice process because it restores social harmony and repairs the harm done to relations of cosmic entities. This stems from the understanding that a living being is a spirit being, who belongs to a cosmological community made up of the physical and metaphysical realms. Within each realm are living entities bound by an interdependent relationship that connects those existing in the physical world and the metaphysical (Gelfand 1973). Hence, African spirituality is considered a sacred realm that is interconnected with the daily experiences of people such that their religion, culture and society are inseparable (Olupona 2011). It is an embodiment through which living beings relate with the primary source of life, i.e. the Supreme Being in relation to all entities in the cosmological community (Paris 1993).

From this perspective, there is no differentiation between the religious and secular spheres because it is inconceivable to imagine life outside of its connection to the cosmological realm (Olupona 2011). Paris (1993) points out that neither humanity nor nature can exist in isolation but in relation to the universe which inhabits eternal spirits. As such, when violence occurs, justice is a process of repairing damage that occurs to relations of entities in both the physical and metaphysical realm. Among the studied communities, people believe that misfortunes are caused by harmful actions that disrupt the cosmological balance in their environment. For instance, when one's actions cause harm to others, it leaves people with *kugunun'una mumoyo* (grumbling spirit). *Mai* Mukwa said,

> *Firo yemwana wangu haigamuchirike kuti aive akatarirwa mazuva mashoma uye kuti ndiyo yaive firo yake. Nanhasi mhuri yese hapana ati amboigashira nyaya yekufa kwemukomana* (It is difficult to accept the way my son died and to think that he was meant to have a short life. Up to this day the whole family has not come to terms with the matter).

The pain of losing a loved one destroys the human spirit. So, I inquired from *mai* Mukwa how relations of people are since her son's ordeal. She stated,

> Things have remained tense, and there are some who caused the harms *vave kupenga* (facing psychological challenges). So even though *vanhu vanenge vakuita sevave kukanganwa* (people may seem to have forgotten about the incident) and have been silenced, the unresolved issues have a way of coming out, like *izvi zvevanhu vave kupenga* (through the insanity of those possessed by the avenging spirit).

Babamukuru Mutyairi weighed in on the notion of *kupenga* by saying,

> *Hazvitenderwi kuti uwurayise weropa rako. Unosvibisa nyika nekudeura ropa* (the cosmological community is polluted when blood is spilled). So, *munhu haangorove* (a person's spirit does not just disappear). God created every being and expects it to die of natural causes. But when one orchestrates their murder it means you have played god. And God would not just leave it at that. More so, *vadzimu* (ancestors) are always vicious when fighting for their offspring because it is their role to protect the family.

Munhu haangorove means that when someone has died their living spirit does not vanish into thin air. Death is a rite of passage into the realm of the living dead where one takes on a new role as a guardian to the family among the living dead. But when their spirit is angered it carries bad aura that does not augur well with the tranquillity of the metaphysical realm hence, they get into a state of limbo. This is considered being homeless because when one dies their spirit is expected to rest among *vebwo*. Closely linked to *munhu haangorove* is the proverb *mhosva hairove* which means bad deeds can never be concealed. They always find their way back into people's lives, and therefore, it is important for people in the studied community to maintain good relations by treating each other with dignity. There is a saying *mabasa ako anokutevera* which they used often during our interactions. It means all your deeds will beget returns in your life whether good or bad. Hence, how one relates with people and their environment is key to their own well-being because *munhu vanhu* (a person belongs with people) and *upenyu vanhu* (life is a shared enterprise).

Kupenga is therefore a form of tormenting caused by the avenging spirit of the deceased as it seeks for atonement which allows it to ascend and rest among the living dead. *Ambuya* Meso indicated that *kupenga* was rather a benign attack from the avenging spirits because '*inotogona kuuraya vanhu kuti muzvitsvage* (it may cause death in the family of the wrongdoer to provoke the affected parties to seek for answers)'. I probed her to explain how the deaths occur and she stated,

> *Inouraya* (it kills) in different ways. A direct attack, illness, accidents, suicide etc. The spirit of the deceased sometimes manifests as *ngozi* (avenging spirit) and speaks out through one of the family members that *ndiyo iri kuuraya vanhu* (claim responsibility for the deaths) or the family may consult with spiritualists and get clarity on causes of death or misfortunes. People here consult a lot when they need guidance related to their plans in life or *pundutso* (a pathway to address misfortunes).

The combination of an angered spirit of the deceased and *vadzimu vakatsamwa* (angered ancestors) creates a bad aura around the community which is believed to cause misfortunes, discomfort and disharmony. This avenging spirit has legitimate claim for causing havoc in the lives of those who wronged the deceased, and in the studied communities, there seems to be no condemnation against the attacks of the spirit. Instead, the affected parties are expected to take action to atone because failure to do so may cause discomfort to many others who may not have been party to the bad action. Honwana (1997) has described this phenomenon as social pollution—a form of hovering and restless spiritual entity that disrupts the cosmic balance between entities in the physical and metaphysical realms. The bad aura continues to be flared by *kugumbuka kwevanhu* (the heartache or disappointment in people's hearts) which causes them to *reverara* (make utterances to the universe) until the wronged party atones. Thus, justice is exercised through spiritual strife because they believe that *Mwari ndiye anogadzirisa zvose* (Supreme Being can repair all relations). The Supreme Being as the creator has means to transform *unhu hwemunhu aita zvakaipa* (the bad character).

Spiritual tormenting can manifest as misfortunes, like *kurwara* or *kushaya mabasa* (falling ill or failing to find employment). Being unable to find employment when one is at the age when they should be economically active and contributing to their family disrupts the well-being of the community. It raises concerns in the family because they also believe that *kubudirira* (prospering in life) and *maropafadzo* (blessings or fortune) are fruits of the spirits. The universe provides for its people, and the ancestors are key entities in interceding with *Musikavanhu* to bring fortune to their offspring. Ancestors are guardians in the spiritual realm but when one of theirs is angered they turn away from their role of protecting, providing and interceding for the family. Prospering is an indication of favour from the universe when the cosmic relations are in good standing. Hence, the absence of fortune is an indication that there is no harmony. *Babamunini* Mugezo expressed that,

> In our cultural beliefs there are some misfortunes that happen which cannot be explained scientifically for example *unogona kurwara woenda kuchipatara* (you may fall ill) and the doctor fails to find a problem. Or at your workplace you may be accused of something you did not commit. In other instances, your neighbours in your community may accuse you of something or you may lose your livestock. When these misfortunes occur, people tend to seek for answers or solutions by consulting with *n'anga* or *maporofita* (traditional healers and prophets) and they may be told *kunzi pane mhosva iripo inoda kuripirwa* (they will be advised that there is a wrongdoing that needs appeasement).

Fortune as described above entails having good health, source of living and living in harmony with others. But when one falls ill, fails to find employment or cannot live well with others their lives will be in disarray. The imbalance is repaired by performing rituals and ceremonies that restore harmony among cosmic entities. This captures the humanistic and spiritual values of *Hunhu*, because *upenyu vanhu* (life is a shared enterprise).

Cleansing, Rituals and Remedy

A war waged between the spirit of the dead and the person/s responsible for the death plays out in the spiritual realm causing new forms of violence, especially among the families of the parties involved. The conflict transcends to the spiritual realm and ceases to be a political contestation, rather a metaphysical contestation where the assailants and family of the deceased battles until remedies are rendered. This contestation can take a much longer time frame, one that is not linear, but the wronged family continues to believe in the power of the universe to cause all things to come back together. Even when one may have been killed in 2008, the effects are not bound by time or space, the spirit of the dead can avenge through to future generations, because the life of the dead, living and future unborn is interconnected. This interconnection keeps human experiences alive and the demand for justice vivid; hence, some often return to the community to atone. In this section, I discuss some of the cultural rituals, processes and ceremonies that are crucial to the studied communities when dealing with violence.

De Coppet (2002) considers rituals as values that create, maintain, inform or transform a society's cultural identity and social relations. Rituals provide a lens to understand the continuities and discontinuities of the values held by social groupings and how they inform their realities. Parkin (2002: 18) adds that rituals are 'formulaic spatiality carried out by groups of people who are conscious of its imperative or compulsory nature and who may or may not further inform this spatiality with spoken words'. From this definition, Klingbeil (2007: 15) establishes that a ritual is (i) situated in spatiality (applicable in a specific context), (ii) it has a formulaic component meaning method that is acceptable within its context, and (iii) societal function that is recognised by the concerned grouping. These three features of rituals are used to give understanding to the practices observed in the studied communities relating to addressing violence, which include *nyaradzo*, *magadziro*, *chenura*, *kubvunzira* and *kuripira ngozi*.

Nyaradzo

In the socio-cultural customs of the studied communities, *nyaradzo* is a memorial ceremony performed a few weeks after burial, to commemorate and remember the life of the deceased. During this ceremony friends, family, relatives and community members join the bereaved family to pay their respect to the deceased and to console the grieving family. *Mai* Mukwa explained,

> We performed *nyaradzo* for my son and put a tombstone on his grave, but this ceremony was not well attended, people were still afraid due to the political atmosphere. When we performed *kurova guva* a year after his burial it was well attended the fear had dissipated. During this ceremony we made prayers to the spirit realm requesting for his spirit to return and look after the family. It is led by family elders who can connect and address the spirit of the deceased.

Nyaradzo is an important ceremony in the studied communities because of the collective efforts that bring people together to mourn, comfort the bereaved and remember the deceased. During this ceremony, the family of the deceased also distribute personal belongings of their loved ones which they call *kugovera nhumbi dzomufi*. Personal belongings such as clothes are usually shared among the family, friends and relatives as a token to remember the deceased. This is one way the dead continue to live among the living beings because people have tangible materials that connect them with the deceased.

There are however challenges associated with distributing the belongings of the deceased, especially where the death is unnatural. Some believe that clothing of the deceased may be misused to evoke the spirit of the dead for personal gain. Hence, some limit the persons that are given the belongings and perform prayers or sprinkle sacred herbal mixture that creates a hedge of spiritual protection against any evil actions. Other challenges come with family members competing for the belongings of the deceased, for instance when it is a married woman, her relatives may demand all her household belongings, for example, bed, bedding and kitchen utensils. They would not want a new partner to use her belongings, unless the man picks from within which they call getting *chigara mapfihwa*. On the contrary when it is a man that has died and the woman is young like the spouse of Nherera, she inherits the estate of the deceased, but since the deceased did not own property she continued staying and being supported by her in-laws until the child was 2-year-old. After the two years, she opted to re-marry and decided to leave the child behind as *munyaradzi anotandadza ambuya* (a bringer of peace and solace to the grieving grandmother). Thus, the life of the deceased continues to be witnessed through his offspring.

Mbuya Meso also weighed in on *nyaradzo* by indicating that at her husband's funeral in August 2008, the atmosphere was tense '*hama dzaisaonana*' (people were not on talking terms) because of the anger around his untimely death. Her husband was unlawfully detained for several weeks after being sold out to ZANU-PF elements by his brother, Nakirwai during the electoral violence of May–June 2008. While in prison he was denied access to health care to treat the wounds, he succumbed when the ZANU-PF youths and state security agents raided his home. He was also deprived of food which put his health in a bad state. *Mbuya* Meso was assisted by a human rights lawyer from Harare to get bail for her husband from Buhera police station where he had been detained. Upon his release, he died two months later from complications associated with ill-treatment in prison and pre-existing medical conditions. Hence, the funeral had a tense atmosphere because Nakirwai was being accused of having a hand in the death of his own sibling. It was reported that this brother could not attend the funeral due to fears of being chastised by angry family members.

But at the *nyaradzo* Nakirwai reached to family elders and they organised a *dare akakumbira ruregerero* (where he apologised) for his involvement in political actions that cost the life of his sibling. The act of kukumbira ruregerero among the studied communities means one is remorseful for their conduct. *Babamukuru* Mutyairi explained that,

> *Kana munhu afa hupenyu hwake haungadzorerwa pakare* (When a person dies, we cannot regain the lost life). But once someone recognises their harm on others, they have a responsibility to atone for their actions.

At the *dare*, the wrongdoer is given the platform to show remorse for the claims being levelled and offer an apology, which is a gesture that the person is remorseful. An apology is symbolic in that there is a sense of acknowledging the harm done and when that has taken place, it becomes easier to establish consensus on the way forward. It paves the way for the wronged party to *nyevenutsa moyo* (the softening of the heart), consequently enabling the conflicting parties to begin to relate better and even appear to be *vanhu vakavandutswa mwoyo* (people with a changed heart), particularly once the *dare* is completed. The resentment does not disappear immediately, but the parties will have curved a path on which to renew their relations with the understanding that *potsi haarwirwe*, which suggests that bad actions should not continue or be used against each other.

Benyera (2014) has also observed that *nyaradzo* was used by civil society organisations, for example Heal Zimbabwe and the traditional leaders to assist several communities in Buhera, to come to terms with the 2008 electoral violence. These memorial ceremonies were widely attended because many people in the community had not been able to observe the burials of their loved ones due to the political tensions that clouded the post-2008 elections. Hence, the *nyaradzo* was an avenue for the local people to talk about the past and iron out issues, especially where allegations of the cause of death were being levelled against fellow community members. In this instance, prior to the ceremony, the aggrieved family were involved in mediation talks with the alleged perpetrators and apology, forgiveness and compensations occurred (for instance, helping to rebuild torched homes), which enabled the community members and even family members to rebuild relationships (Benyera 2014). Benyera (2014) observed that though the confessions that occurred during the *nyaradzo* were done publicly and the events were attended by the local police, no arrests were made. What was important for some of the affected families was to repair relations because they still need to find ways to coexist and one of which is by engaging on the issues that occurred.

Magadziro

Linked to *nyaradzo* is the *magadziro* or *kurova guva* ritual mentioned by *mai* Mukwa earlier. It is also known as *bona*, *bora* or *bota* and performed after about one rainy season from the time the deceased has been buried. In some Christian families, they only unveil a tombstone while other families also perform *magadziro*. *Kurova guva* is a traditional ceremony in which the spirit of the deceased is welcomed back into the family as a guardian among the ancestral community. Here, a goat or sheep is used as an offering during the ceremony which involves brewing of traditional beer and all-night celebrations (*pungwe*). The processes followed during the *bona* ritual were explained by Chief Ngani as follows,

> The horn from the cow or goat used in the ritual is kept in the homestead. We place it on the edge on top of the main door of a kitchen hut that has thatched roof. It serves as remembrance of return of the spirit of the deceased. In our customs when a person dies, it means we have been separated physically but we remain connected in spirit. The person returns as a guardian spirit [ancestral member] looking after the family. When we perform *kurova guva* we use traditional beer and it symbolizes the path of the spirit of the deceased as it returns into the homestead. This beer is prepared by elderly men and women in the community or friends of the deceased. It is made of pearl millet, finger millet and soaked finger millet. When the ritual is being performed the sacrificial animal will be referred to using the name and clan praise name of the deceased, calling it to return.

Before the ceremony commences, the animal is brought into the compound and tied to a tree. The whole family and relatives gather about the tree, and the selected family representative leads the ceremony by pouring traditional beer on the animal and the ground for the ancestors to drink. They also make use of *bute* (snuff) which is sprinkled on the ground as they chant to the ancestors, moving about the compound, inviting the spirit of the deceased back into the family. The rest of the attendants will be singing, dancing and chanting praise to the ancestors. *Vatete* Chama explained the song and dance session saying,

> A song that people sing while moving around the sacrificial animal for the spirit of the deceased to return is called *chikombe*, which is accompanied by playing two small drums called *tusindi*. Other drums that are played include *mutumba* which you play while standing and *jenje* a bass drum that amplifies the percussion. The *jenje* is played while standing using two sticks called *miyembo*. The congregants will be dancing around a calabash

> with the traditional beer and singing songs such as *majekunje*. The sacrificial animal will also be responding to the rhythm of the music and dance and people will be revering it. When we sing *chikombe* [another ritual song] in some cases we will not express any words just whirling sounds.

It is expected that once the spirit of the deceased has descended (*wasvika mumusha*), the animal bows down and one of the family members gets into a trance. When this occurs, the deceased's spirit will address the gathering through the host (*homwe*), an act that symbolises the return of the spirit being as a guardian that will remain in the compound protecting and providing for the family. Where the deceased is aggrieved and has not been atoned, the family elders also charge their spirit to continue fighting for justice.

Chenura

When the death of a person has been orchestrated by another person, *chenura* is required to cleanse the deceased from the bad aura that surrounds unlawful killing. The local chiefs mentioned that they must first report the murder to the police and allow criminal proceedings to occur. But, in accordance with their local customs, *chenura* (cleansing) should also be done to disinfect the community from the bad aura associated with the unlawful killing of a person.

This cleansing ritual and ceremony involves the slaughtering of an animal (cattle, goat or lamb) and smearing of the animal's blood mixed with traditional herbs at the spot where the person died. Here, the wrongdoers or their families are expected by the local chief to offer an animal to the ancestors of the land (*masvikiro enzvimbo*) and to ask for forgiveness for polluting the environment. The animal is slaughtered according to custom, and the blood of the bull is poured to the ground as the *homwe* (host to the spirit medium) chants to the ancestors asking for forgiveness. This is followed by *pungwe* (celebration ceremony) in which community members gather all night to sing, dance and share in traditional beer and eat the meat from the slaughtered bull. Part of that meat is also put in a traditional plate and placed *mumba mesvikiro* (the hut of the ancestral spirit) together with traditional beer for the ancestors to feast. *Mai* Mukwa indicated that,

> My heart is not settled because the family has not been able to visit the place where my son was murdered in 2008. His spirit has not been able to rest well among *vebwo* (departed clan members) because we have not been able to go to the spot where he was murdered, and the perpetrators have not yet cleansed his spirit. Even the local leaders are afraid to initiate the process because my son was murdered by ZANU PF militias who had been given orders by high ranking political figures. It pains me that my son's life was cut short in a gruesome manner, but even in death his spirit has not rested.

The cleansing required by *mai* Mukwa is *chenura,* and it is performed to exorcise the environment from the bad aura associated with spilling of human blood. She reported that her son's spirit has remained in limbo tormenting community members around the spot he was murdered because *ropa remufi* (the blood of the deceased) has polluted the *ivhu* (land, territory, environment). This pollution disrupts harmony among cosmic beings; hence, cleansing is required to disinfect the social environment from the bad aura of an aggrieved spirit of the deceased. The locals believe that *chenura* consoles an aggrieved spirit enabling the spirit of the deceased to join the ancestral family and commence duties as a guardian among *vadzimu nenyika* (ancestors of the land). This practice thus facilitates psychosocial and spiritual healing for the affected communities.

The cleansing ritual is usually performed with the assistance of a traditional healer or prophets. These spiritual ritual performers make use of livestock such as hens, cattle, goats and sheep, which they slaughter as an offering to the spiritual realm. The prophet takes the blood of the sacrificed animal back to the family holding the cleansing ceremony and uses it to wash the people, which often marks their freedom from spiritual bondage. In other instances, the animal is taken to the mountains, or bush and incense burning or *bute* (snuff) is thrown to the ground as chants or prayers are made before letting the animal loose to wander the world (*kupepereka nenyika*). This act symbolises the detachment of spiritual burden. What can be observed from the above is a striking similarity of procedures and materials used by both the African apostolic religious leaders, i.e. prophets and the African traditional religious leaders, for example *homwe* (host of the spirit medium) or *n'anga* (traditional healer).

Chenura when performed by traditional healers they use traditional herbs and *bute* (snuff) to call upon the spirit of the deceased. The traditional healer burns sacred herbs at the scene of the incident and puts snuff on the ground, which enables the healer to calm the spirit of the deceased and guide it back to the place where remains of the deceased were buried. People in the studied communities still bury remains of their loved ones in their rural homesteads. Thus, *chenura* is done to take the spirit of the deceased to the rural homestead so that it finds a place of rest in the grave where the body of the person was buried.

At a focus group meeting with community members in Buhera district, they described that some people who were killed in the violence that has been occurring in their community are reported to have been thrown into the Ruti and Tsanzaguru dam. *Babamukuru* Mutyairi said,

> Whenever there is violence in this community people disappear [forced disappearances] and that is a very difficult experience for one to go through their life not knowing what became of their beloved one. It pains us a lot to know that there are people who were dumped in Tsanzaguru and Ruti dams but we can never know for sure if any of those people are our relative. Some people have consulted [*kubvunzira*] but the issue can only be resolved when the government performs rituals to cleanse our territory.

The dumping of people's remains in water bodies is a cause of concern for the studied communities because of the pollution it creates to their social environment. Some community members reported that they have stopped fishing or using water from the said bodies because of the pollution that has occurred. It puts spiritual and psychological strain on the local communities because they are deprived of the socio-economic benefits afforded by their natural resources. *Chenura* is still required to cleanse the dams from the bad aura they associate with aggrieved spirits of improperly handled remains of deceased persons.

Where the remains of the deceased have not been found, family members usually consult to establish if they are dead or alive. If they establish that their loved one has died but without a trace, they bury *musoro wemombe* (a head of a cow) in place of the body. This symbolic burial is done to provide the family with a grave site where they can go to and speak *zviri pamoyo pavo* (the burdens on their heart) regarding the whereabouts of the deceased's remains. It is believed that doing so invites the ancestral community to assist in locating the wandering spirit of their loved ones and possibly a place where their remains lie. When it is not possible to find any remains, being able to visit the place where their life was taken allows the family to bring back the spirit to the homestead to rest among *vebwo* (the ancestral family). Here, the ceremony to bring back the spirit is performed on the symbolic grave that has been put in the homestead, thus giving the family spiritual solace that enables them to manage the loss better.

Kubvunzira

Kubvunzira, also known as *gata* or kufamba in the studied communities, is a consultation process to obtain the truth and solutions on unclear or unpleasant experiences. In *kufamba*, people consult from spiritualists, such as n'anga or maporofita (prophets), after encountering problems that are out of the ordinary such as *kupenga* or *kupondwa kwemunhu* (the murder of someone). *Babamunini* Mugezo mentioned that,

> *Vatete pavakavigwa* (when my aunt was buried [referring to *vatete* Rutendo]) the atmosphere was tense, and I am certain *vana sekuru* did not just let it go, *vakafamba* (they consulted).

The indication that *vana sekuru* did not just let it go is that some of the parties involved in the murder of his aunt are reported to be experiencing spiritual strife. The ringleader and group members who orchestrated the violence that he witnessed in 2008 are known to the community and police but were never arrested. Instead, community members in recent years have been observing manifestations of spiritual and psychosocial challenges on the assailants. *Babamunini* Mugezo shared that,

> One guy *akupenga* (he has gone made), and many others no longer sleep in their homes because they are haunted. One of the haunted guys is said to have resorted to sleeping in the bush in a nearby mountain and at one point he was beaten by a snake.

He described these manifestations being faced by the assailants as *kurumwa nechokuchera* (facing the wrath of their evil deeds) because this group is known to have terrorised many in their village, *zvakagumbutsa vari pasi* (which angered those beneath us referring to ancestral spirits who occupy their environment) and *Musikavanhu* or *Nyadenga* (God). These assailants are reportedly facing the wrath of *mweya wengozi* (avenging spirits), which emanates from the angered and wounded spirits of many people that were affected by their acts of terror.

Kufamba that he mentioned means people sought spiritual help to address their grief and to raise the spirit of *vatete* to come back and revenge. It is believed that some people are timid on earth as well as when they die; hence, nudging or evoking the wrath of other ancestors called *varwi vehondo* (fighting spirits) assists the deceased's spirit in fighting. He added that,

> In most cases those who kill immediately do what is known as *kutsipika kuti munhu avauraya asamuka* (scattering sacred portions on the grave of the deceased to suppress the spirit of the dead from rising). So, *kuno bvunzira* is a process of finding out if *pakatsipikwa paguva remunhu* (if the grave has been tempered with) and if so *vobvisa kutsipikwa kuya kuti munhu amuke* (they get a remedy to undo the actions of the person who tempered with the grave).

In a sense, the family will be gathering remedies to strengthen the spirit of the deceased to avenge the wrongdoers. The *n'anga* or *maporofita* can instruct them to buy certain objects and ingredients to perform a ritual to arm the person; for example, the family may be asked to buy *bakatwa* (a small knife) which is revered to the ancestors so the deceased can use as a weapon to revenge. These actions give justice to the family and the deceased because the spiritual realm enables them to bring back the wrongdoers to doing good unto others. It informs their understanding of justice as *kuringanisa* (restoring), *kuenzanisa* (making equal or making amends) and *kuranga* (instilling discipline) usually through spiritual strife. Restoration refers to the renewal of human essence that comes with retaining an equilibrium among cosmic beings. Undergoing spiritual strife puts one under justice because they consider it to be '*mujere rako wega ratongwa nedenga*' (the Supreme Being has arrested their spirit which makes their state of being worse off than inmates in a state prison). Arguably, the tormenting pushes one to a point of *kuzvininipisa* (it humbles you) because to end the torture you must work with others and atone.

Several research participants acknowledged that some of their family members have consulted with both the prophets and traditional healers to establish the whereabouts of their loved ones, especially those that disappeared without a trace. There were reports also that *kubvunzira* could be used by parties who committed acts of violence as either a means to establish the whereabouts of those they harmed or to disempower avenging spirits and address karma.

In this instance, the perpetrator may no longer be aware of the identities of the persons they wronged or the location of *kumusha kwavo* (their village of origin). Knowing the village of origin of wronged parties or their identities enables the wrongdoer to approach remaining relatives and perform redress which ends their spiritual strife. *Kubvunzira* in this instance is performed through consulting with spiritualists who can establish the remedy that could be used to end the spiritual strife. In some cases, when the remedy is too complex for example appeasing the avenging spirit with a human sacrifice, some parties often opt for intermediary remedies such as *kurasirira mweya*, which is a performance to exorcise the avenging spirit by disposing it on another entity. But this only resolves the issue temporarily. Hence, most parties are required to appease the avenging spirit by compensating with cattle to relatives of the deceased, which is discussed below.

Kuripira ngozi

Kuripira ngozi (appeasing the avenging spirit) is a ritual that is done to offer compensation and appeasement to the spirit of the deceased in the case of murder. This tradition-based practice is still considered a useful remedy in the studied communities. During a focus group meeting with traditional leaders in Mudzi, chief Dande described the practice of *ngozi* as follows,

> If a person experiences an unlawful death, the spirit of the deceased comes back to haunt those accused of causing the death. This spirit *unonogara munhu* (occupies the body of another person) within the family of the accused and speaks out its demands, which should be met for the tormenting to stop. At times, the spirit can start off by causing misfortunes and strange ordeals to the family of the accused and people usually go *kunobvunzira* (consulting with spiritualists) so that they get a way to address the occurrences. During these consultations, the spirit of the deceased often makes its demands known and, it usually requires an appeasement.

Ambuya Meso pointed out that,

> Appeasing an avenging spirit is the most complicated thing especially where the victim is male because they may need to be paid off with a woman. If the person died a bachelor or without a child they may insist of being appeased with a woman who can bear children for him with one of his brothers so that he has his own offspring. Sometimes the woman will be married off to the family to bear a child then leave it behind and return to her own life, but others insist on a permanent arrangement. The proper thing is n'anga (traditional healer) should evoke the spirit of the deceased to speak and make its demands known and, where possible the parties can negotiate and the spirit could state a certain number of cattle as the required appeasement.

A challenge with the *kuripira ngoz*i practice comes when the spirit of the deceased demands to be compensated with a woman, which human rights activists have challenged as human sacrifices. This similar challenge was observed by Victor Igreja et al. (2008) in Mozambique with the issue of *magamba* spirits after the civil war. *Magamba* spirits plural for *gamba* (meaning soldier) is a phenomenon associated with the rupture of an avenging spirit of a deceased soldier that possessed another person mostly women in the physical realm and demanded redress including compensation with a wife for the injustices incurred by deceased male soldiers (Igreja 2012). Thompson (2016) argues that in many parts of central Mozambique just like Zimbabwe, *vanhu vatema* (African being) believe that the undignified death of an individual (including improper handling of remains) requires redress through rituals.

Magamba spirits are, arguably, a holistic avenue of redress that has been used to advance transitional justice by the local communities in Mozambique (Thompson 2016). Igreja et al. (2008) recognised the rupture of *magamba* spirits and accompanying redress measures as performances that contributed to the renewal of the human essence both in the physical and metaphysical sense. As such, the *magamba* spirits must be understood from the cosmological relations that African beings have as interdependent entities which makes it an avenue for psychosocial healing among violence-stricken communities (Igreja et al. 2008). It enabled broken communities in central Mozambique to perform healing ceremonies and repair network of relations thereby strengthening the foundation for building their collective future.

Several research participants indicated that the old tradition of the *ngozi* practice involved appeasement with a woman, when the deceased is male, but in recent times the common means has been to offer cattle, indicating that their customs evolve and are created by people to suit their needs and changes to their environment. The participants explained that what contributed to the changes is the constitutional legalities around child marriages, thus an adaptation to their sociopolitical environment. This has presented challenges among families battling ngozi as they have to establish alternatives to human offerings, which is no longer feasible.

A recent case where a girl was used as compensation to appease the avenging spirit (*ngozi*) occurred in Nyanga district in Manicaland Province, where an old man used his underage granddaughter to pay for the murder that had been committed by a member of his family (Zhakata 2017). This incident was however not related to political violence. More so, once the traditional authorities of their community discovered it, they ordered the parties to dissolve the arrangement. The matter also went to the magistrate's court, and the guardians were charged for the unlawful use of a female person under the age of 18 years in marital arrangements

(Zhakata 2017). In the studied communities, *mweya wengozi* has been observed but I did not hear reports of appeasements made yet relating to the electoral violence of 2000–2008.

Benyera (2014) has written extensively on the case of appeasing the avenging spirit (*ngozi*) of Moses Chokuda who was murdered on political grounds in 2008 in Gokwe, Midlands Province. The deceased's remains could not be buried for over two years because his spirit demanded justice, of which the perpetrators took responsibility for their actions by upholding customary procedures of redress (*The Standard* 2011). Father of one of the accused, who was a governor in Midlands province, compensated the aggrieved family with at least 20 heads of cattle and USD15,000 to appease the avenging spirit of the late Chokuda (*The Standard* 2011). The essence of appeasement is to give tangible compensation that improves the conditions of the affected family especially because they would have lost a member that could be contributing to their well-being. Nyathi (2015) adds that the African people in Zimbabwe are devoted to maintaining the harmonious continuation of the cosmological community (physical and metaphysical realms) because that is the essence of their humanity, which guarantees the existence and expansion of their lineage. It is against this backdrop that *ngozi* is appreciated by the studied communities as an avenue of dealing with unnatural deaths.

There are social and economic benefits in using the *ngozi* practice among the local communities (Benyera 2014). Compensation in the form of cattle, goat and sheep can be used for socio-cultural activities including rituals, ceremonies and celebrations. Livestock is also used for food providing meat and milk for the families, while the animal hide is used as seating matts. Cattle is also used for agricultural and domestic activities; for example cattle-drawn plough enables the people to till their farms, while cow dung provides manure and is also used to polish the house floors. Livestock is also used for trade, for example when people do not have money, they can exchange a goat, lamb or hen for food supplies and clothing. In some cases, the rural people have sold their livestock to raise money to pay for goods and services such as sending their children to school or getting medical treatment.

Ngozi has functional and materialistic value to studied communities because once a plan for restitution has been made or compensation has been offered, an equilibrium among the conflicting parties is fostered. The balance is forged in that the spirit of the deceased gets calm and can join the 'living dead'. Resultantly, social harmony is established between the physical and metaphysical realms. Moreover, the family of the deceased have tangible resources to use for their upkeep. For example, *mai* Mukwa reported that the death of her son had brought financial and emotional burden on her family. Her son was the breadwinner and he left behind a wife and infant baby, whom she has had to look after, but she is struggling because of a lack of employment.

The symbolic value of appeasing *ngozi* is that once an offender has accepted responsibility for the harm done, he/she is usually given time to raise the resources required to appease the spirit of the deceased. Following this practice, the offender is not sent to jail but remains within the community working towards raising the resources needed for compensation (Benyera 2014). As such, the offender can remain looking after his/her own family because sending someone to jail often adds burden on the community. Usually when one has been sent to jail, the relatives are left to look after the family of the offender, which can be burdensome financially, as many of the people are living on limited economic resources. More so, since compensation involves livestock which has high economic value in the studied communities, the cost of acquiring the required amount of cattle serves as deterrence because normally it drags the whole family to raise the funds. There is a sense of fear for *mweya wengozi* and this pushes people to commit to living in harmony.

Conclusion

Justice witnessed in the studied communities is the manifestation of bad omen that is associated with the bad behaviour, which they regard as *kurumwa nechokuchera* (reaping a seed of their violent actions). They believe that when *vadzimu vave kutonga* (the ancestors are giving judgement), it is no longer in the jurisdiction of the living but of the living dead who will only turn things around when they are appeased. Whether it takes decades to be resolved the living are not necessarily bothered because the battle is not in their hands. It is now playing out in a realm they have no control over, but totally trust to have the authority to retain the required cosmic balance by tormenting the one who misbehaved until they return to the co-values of the community, especially *kuva vanhu vanozvininipisa* (being humble), *vanodzoreka* (having a teachable spirit), *nekukumbira ruregerero pavanenge vakanganisira vamwe* (and seeking for atonement when they have wronged others).

For as long as the afflicted parties feel wounded or aggrieved, the bad spell continues to torment. It takes *kunyevenutsa moyo yavo* for the cosmic balance to be retained, which occurs on both ends, where the afflicted chooses to forgive and the afflicting party takes responsibility for their actions because *potsi haarwirwe*. This includes owning up to their actions, apologising and appeasing the wounded spirit, which forms the exercise of rebuilding relations. The longer one takes to come forth and address issues, the more wrath and problems they face. Justice is a continuous strife in which the universe reconditions relations and behaviours of afflicted communities. Wrongdoers are rehabilitated through strife, especially when they seem to be stubborn. Some people may be arrogant unto death, but the battle continues in their bloodline; hence, there is a sense of moral obligation to repair things to avoid depriving yourself and offspring *maropafadzo emhuri* (ancestral benefits).

References

Benyera, E. 2014. *Debating the Efficacy Transitional Justice Mechanisms: The Case of National Healing in Zimbabwe*. Doctoral Dissertation, University of South Africa, Pretoria.

De Coppet, D. (ed.). 2002. *Understanding Rituals*. London: Routledge.

Gale, R., and A. Pruss. 1999. A New Cosmological Argument. *Religious Studies* 35 (4): 461–476.

Gelfand, M. 1973. *The Genuine Shona: Survival of Values of an African Culture*. Gwelo: Mambo Press.

Gelfand, M. 1981. *Ukama*. Gwelo: Mambo Press.

Honwana, A.M. 1997. Healing for Peace: Traditional Healers and Post-War Reconstruction in Southern Mozambique. *Peace and Conflict: Journal of Peace Psychology* 3 (3): 293–305.

Igreja, V. 2012. Multiple Temporalities in Indigenous Justice and Healing Practices in Mozambique. *International Journal of Transitional Justice* 6 (3): 404–422.

Igreja, V., B. Dias-Lambranca, and A. Richters. 2008. Gamba Spirits, Gender Relations, and Healing in Post-Civil War Gorongosa, Mozambique. *Journal of the Royal Anthropological Institute* 14 (2): 353–371.

Klingbeil, G.A. 2007. *Bridging the Gap: Ritual and Ritual Texts in the Bible.* Winona Lake, IN: Eisenbrauns.

Meldrum, A. 2000. *Opposition Reports New Attacks as White Farm Owner Killed*. Available from https://www.irishtimes.com/news/opposition-reports-new-attacks-as-white-farm-owner-killed-1.268835. Accessed 2 December 2019.

Nigosian, S.A. 1994. *World Faiths*. New York: St. Martin's Press.

Nyathi, P. 2015. *Ngozi: An African Reality…Ensuring Social Justice and Fairness*. Available from http://www.herald.co.zw/ngozi-an-african-reality-ensuring-social-justice-and-fairness/. Accessed 24 November 2019.

Olupona, J.K. 2011. The Changing Face of African Christianity: Reverse Mission in Transnational and Global Perspectives. In *Transnational Africa and Globalization*, ed. M.O. Okome and O. Vaughan, 179–194. New York: Palgrave Macmillan.

Paris, J. 1993. The Spirituality of African Peoples. *Journal of Black Theology in S.A.* 7 (2): 114–124.

Parkin, D. 2002. Ritual as Spatial Direction and Bodily Division. In *Understanding Rituals*, ed. D. De Coppet, 11–25. London: Routledge.

The Standard. 2011. *Chokuda Case: Avenging Spirits Exact Justice?* Available from https://www.thestandard.co.zw/2011/10/30/chokuda-case-avenging-spirits-exact-justice/. Accessed 7 November 2019.

Thompson, K.G. 2016. Indigenous Transitional Justice in Perspective: The Case of Mozambique. *Small Wars Journal*. Available from http://smallwarsjournal.com/print/47110. Accessed 8 August 2019.

Zhakata, A. 2017. *Girl (4) Paid to Ngozi*. Available from http://manicapost.co.zw/girl-4-paid-to-ngozi/. Accessed 7 November 2019.

5

Discourses on Transitional Justice: A National Dialogue

Abstract Transitional justice is a contested sociopolitical concept that pose a lot of challenges for violence-stricken communities in Africa. Increasingly transitional justice processes have ignited contending approaches, goals and policies, which range from Western-centred legal frameworks (focusing on criminal prosecution) to broader African justice processes that seek to rebuild interpersonal relations. In this chapter, these aspects are explored in relation to the deliberations that occurred between 2016 and 2017 during the public hearings on the Peace Commission in Zimbabwe. It establishes that various people hold varying meanings of what would count for justice to be served. Therefore, a one-size-fits-all approach to transitional justice in Zimbabwe will not be adequate. An enabling environment that accommodates various views of justice is required.

Keywords Public hearings · Commission · Human rights · Reconciliation · Peace · Truth · Apology · Forgiveness

R. Murambadoro, *Transitional Justice in Africa*, Development, Justice and Citizenship, https://doi.org/10.1007/978-3-030-48092-9_5

Introduction

During my field trips in 2016 and 2017, I had the opportunity to attend public hearings held by government to deliberate the draft bill of the National Peace and Reconciliation Commission (NPRC). My doctoral project had begun the previous year, and in my research proposal, I had written that this commission was dormant. Well at least since 2013 when the new Constitution was enacted paving way for the establishment of independent commissions and one of which was the NPRC.

Chapter 12 of the 2013 amended Constitution of Zimbabwe set out independent commissions that should be established by government to protect human rights, promote democracy, healing, civic trust and cohesion (Constitution of Zimbabwe 2013). These were the Zimbabwe Anti-Corruption Commission (ZACC), Zimbabwe Electoral Commission (ZEC), Zimbabwe Human Rights Commission (ZHRC), Zimbabwe Gender Commission, Zimbabwe Media Commission and the National Peace and Reconciliation Commission (NPRC) (Constitution of Zimbabwe 2013). In 2015, when I began my research, most of these commissions had been set up except for the NPRC which raised tensions between the government, civil society and other interested parties in the country. One challenge with the absence of this commission was that it had a pre-determined lifespan of ten years, which commenced in 2013 when the new constitution was adopted. Hence, when the government had spent almost three years from 2013 to 2015 screening candidates suitable to serve as commissioners it compromised the lifespan of the commission (*National Transitional Justice Working Group* 2016).

A draft bill to enact the work of the commission was gazetted by the executive on 18 December 2015 but many civic groups challenged government indicating contradictions with provisions of the constitution (*Zimbabwe Human Rights NGO Forum* 2016). One of the issues raised was that the bill had given the executive unrestrained power to interfere in investigations of the commission and this provision contravened constitutional requirements (Reeler 2016). A 2016 report made by the National Transitional Justice Working Group (NTJWG) after reviewing the bill labelled it a lame and whimsical tool set to satisfy views of insensitive politicians. But since the bill had been gazetted, the general public was expected to weigh in their views on the initiative through public hearings. In this chapter, I focus on the deliberations that took place during sessions of the NPRC hearings giving attention to the competing, converging and contradicting perspectives that fledged the national discourse around redressing the past.

NPRC Hearings Without Hearing

My first attendance of the NPRC bill public hearings was in Chinhoyi in April 2016. The government notice in the local newspapers had indicated the Cooksey Memorial Hall in the city centre as the venue for the hearings in Chinhoyi. However, when my assistant Nesu and I got to the hall, it was empty. Upon inquiring from some city council officials who were around about the new possible venue, we established that the meeting had been moved to Chaedza Hall (a community hall in a nearby *rukesheni* or high-density residential area).

Fortunately, we got to the new venue before the session had begun but the building was quickly filling up. Nesu and I managed to squeeze in and found a spot to sit in the middle section. A member of parliament in the portfolio committee chairing the session vaChisvo opened the meeting by informing the congregants the purpose of the public hearings. He explained that the commission had been set to promote *runyararo* (peace) and reconciliation among communities affected by violence. VaChisvo added that such a commission is required for the country to move forward in harmony as it helps people to come together and work towards correcting any things that may be preventing people from working and walking in one accord. But for such a commission to be able to work well, it needed to be empowered by *bumbiro remutemo* (Bill then Act) which determines the proceedings of the commission and the expected results. He read a summary of the Bill and the constitutional provisions of the NPRC, regarding its functions and then opened the floor for the public to share their views.

What caught my attention while listening to vaChisvo was that he did not use the concept transitional justice; instead, he selected Shona words to express the terms peace and reconciliation. He termed peace *runyararo* and reconciliation *kuregererana*, and these translations convey varying meanings around the ideas held by state officials in relation to the outcomes of the commission. *Runyararo* can literary mean silence, which is the absence of noise. To address noise, people needed to figure out: Who made the noise, what makes the noise and what constitute to noise? *Runyararo* can refer to a form of embodiment in which the mind, body and spirit are in harmony, resulting to the phenomenon of *kugadzikana mumoyo* (a settled heart). However, I never got the sense that this second meaning of *runyararo* was the intended use of the term by this official. I express some reservations around this meaning because vaChisvo stated reconciliation as *kuregererana* (forgiving each other), *kukanganwirana* (letting go of the past) and *kugarisana* (living together), which he mentioned would enable people to move past the disruptions that have occurred in the country.

It is important to note that, there are no Shona words for transitional justice, and this could be a reason why vaChisvo used vernacular terms for peace *runyararo* and reconciliation (*kuregererana, kukanganwirana* and *kugarisana*). Hayner (2010) argues that including the notion of reconciliation in peacebuilding processes often leads state actors to assume that reconciliation is integral or even the primary reason for implementing transitional justice, which is not the case. She adds that following the example of the TRC in South Africa, several states have implemented varying forms of reconciliation commissions without fully grasping the purpose and implications of the concept.

In its narrow sense, reconciliation is regarded as coexistence, 'the condition under which citizens can trust each other as citizens again' (Bosire 2006: 27; Wielenga et al. 2015). On the contrary, the broad definition of reconciliation prescribes the engagement of conflicting parties as humans-in-relation, restoration of broken relationships, accountability, as well as cooperation among community members in developing a future that supports the well-being of all (Lederach 1997; Wielenga et al. 2015). Furthermore, a distinction can be made between national and interpersonal reconciliation. National reconciliation refers to the processes that are facilitated by the government or other state actors that aim to foster civic trust, unity and national healing (Bosire 2006: 28). In contrast, interpersonal reconciliation focuses on restoring broken relations among individuals who are either intra or inter-communal (Wielenga et al. 2015).

These variations between the narrow or broad and national or interpersonal definitions of reconciliation were visible in the deliberations that occurred in the public hearings as well as with local communities. Research participants expressed reconciliation as *yananiso* (bringing back together), *kugadzirisana* (fixing things), *kutaurirana* (engaging in dialogue) and *kuringanisa* (making amends or restoring things), terms which explain that the conflicting parties come together to establish an amicable solution. On the contrary, the words *kuregererana* (forgiving each other), *kukanganwirana* (letting go of the past) and *kugarisana* (living together) describe a process that is less involving and leading towards amnesia. Arguably, such expressions by a government official were leaning towards political reconciliation and national cohesion but not interpersonal harmony.

When the floor was opened for attendees to share their thoughts, I soon realised that the hearings were more of pouring out sessions without anyone hearing the other. My assumption going for the hearings was that people will be engaging in dialogue; instead, some tried to dominate the discussion and seemed to have come with a rehearsed proposition. One middle-aged woman *mai* Nyadzwa made the remark,

> Mr Mugabe and Mr Nkomo created a unity government in 1987 to indicate that they had forgiven each other. What else do we need to forgive each other for? *Hatingarambe tichidya sadza chimunya toda riri fresh* (We cannot continue feasting on left over pap, we need something fresh [literal meaning]).

The phrase '*hatingarambe tichidya sadza chimunya toda riri* fresh' is a figurative expression that means there is no need to look to the past or dwell on past matters, rather look forward. This suggested that the public hearings were unnecessary because there are no matters to resolve. In her view, the Unity Accord signed in 1987 between leaders of ZANU-PF and ZAPU solidified unity in the country, and there are no issues left to address. It is plausible that for her, political reconciliation was enough for the country to move forward. However, her call seemed to silence the needs of parties that were affected by the *Gukurahundi* massacres, which I covered in my master's research. Many respondents I engaged with for my master's project are still demanding for redress, proper reburials, apology and information on whereabouts of their missing loved ones (Murambadoro 2015). More so, there was sense of lack of empathy in this remark, which many scholars argue is essential for national transitional justice initiatives to be effective (Bosire 2006; Brounéus 2008).

Sekuru Mbaye who is related to one of the officials in the parliamentary committee that chaired the session in Chinhoyi also stated,

> Can you please ensure that the bill is translated to all the local dialects in Zimbabwe so that we can all understand it and be able to contribute more and engage better. You mentioned about reconciliation, but I am not sure what are we reconciling for or about? *Kune hondo here* (is there a war/are we at war)? *Hondo yakapera ngatitarisei zviri mberi, titsvage nzira dzekuti vanhu vararame* (the war ended long back, let's look forward, we need to establish the means for people to live well [the crowd ululated]).

His question on whether there is a war or not raised two intertwined issues (i) timing and (ii) nature of transition. Transitional justice initiatives are often conducted to address a failed state, rogue state, civil war, insurgency, authoritarian rule or gross human rights violations by providing redress and establishing a democratic dispensation (Bosire 2006; Sandoval Villalba 2011). But the term transition is highly contested and gives varying meanings to different contexts. *Sekuru* Mbaye was uncertain whether the state was facing any war and the nature of violence that warranted an initiative such as the peace commission. The crowd ululated suggesting his remarks were a concern shared by many. An official chairing the session interjected and made a remark that there are no right and wrong answers to terms of the commission, the purpose of the hearings was for people to bring out their views and give meaning to the process. Another speaker, Chibwi said,

> Let me tell you, I am a war veteran. I used to cook for ZIPRA and ZANLA forces. I lost my tooth during the liberation struggle but here

> I am today all because of forgiving and letting go. I continue to forgive and encourage others to do the same, just forgive and we move forward.

At the time, Chibwi spoke the cheers increased and the programme chair had to call the attendees back to order. I presume it is understandable that a call to forgive by someone who fought in the liberation struggle would attract the standing ovation she received. Chibwi was a woman in her late 50s and her postulation of forgiveness suggested a deviation from the urge to hold on to unpleasant pasts. This view was contested by other attendees as well as participants in the studied communities who indicated that justice and reconciliation cannot be achieved without *chokwadi* (truth), *kukumbira ruregerero* (asking for forgiveness or apology), *kuwirirana* (mutual understanding), *kuvimbisika* (honesty), *kubvuma mhosva/ukuvuma* (acknowledgement), *kuvandutsa moyo* (change of heart) and *muripo* (compensation).

In accordance with the customary values and norms of the studied communities, an apology is a crucial gesture that can repair broken relationships. It is a natural expectation that when one offends another, there is need to apologise so that people can start to relate with each other again. Thus, the underlying assumption is that an offence breaks the social contract that binds people to live in social harmony. When one offers an apology, it is an act of humbleness and respect for the human dignity that has been violated during the conflict.

Forgiveness is a reciprocal act to an apology in some cases. In other instances, it is fundamental in that it enables the mediators to the conflict to assist conflicting parties to begin discussing the issues that caused the conflict. More so, forgiveness is internal and symbolic. Forgiveness sets the aggrieved free from the pain and heartache, possibly contributing to *kunyevenutsa moyo* (softening the heart), and simultaneously, it sets the wrongdoer free from spiritual bondage because when one has *nyevenutsa moyo* (softened their heart), the ancestors are also able to revoke their vengeance. When one has been forgiven, they are expected to also change in behaviour (*kushanduka pamaitiro*), and the offended party is encouraged not to hold the past against the offender (*potsi haarwire*) or have a grudge (*kuchengeta chigumbu*). This means that forgiveness enables *kuvandutswa kwemoyo yevanhu* (change people's hearts).

Compensation is about pleasing the aggrieved. In this case, the affected party determines the reparations needed to let go and begin to rebuild his/her life. It also has a restraining element in that the offending party sacrifices something to make amends for the wrong committed. This is also seen as the procedure for retaining the balance (*kuyananisa vanhu zvakaringana*). Soliciting the truth about what transpired was reported to be vital in assisting the affected community to get closure.

Literature identifies various forms of truth, including forensic truth (factual and measurable), personal truth (one's narrative or account of things), social truth (narrative established through interaction) and healing or reconciliatory truth (public knowledge or national narrative) (Boraine 2009; Hamber and Kibble 1999). Each of these forms of truth determines how people understand what has occurred to them. From the interactions I had with participants in the local communities, truth was explained as getting intel information on the questions they have. This information is for personal closure and not necessarily evidence to be used before the court of law or to establish a national memory.

Given that the violence that occurred has been committed by people within the same community, some of whom are family members, the truth that is desired, therefore, is information that enables the divided families to rebuild relations. Brounéus (2008) believes that acquiring details on what has happened to a loved one can have therapeutic benefits to individuals and the community because it gives people information that allows them to process the trauma and burden, they may be experiencing. Villa-Vicencio (2007) adds that truth can assist in creating the space for open dialogue and honesty which enables communities to come to terms with their burdened spirit. The research participants described that if the offender opens to them how things turned out the way they did, they would be able to share their experiences on how it affected them. This suggests that the dialogue process of establishing what transpired will enable the conflicting parties to understand how they have both been affected by the incident, rendering the notion of justice as *kunzwana nhunha* (listening to troubling issues). Linked to *kunzwana nhunha* is the principle of *kunzwirana* (empathy), which suggests that *chokwadi* (truth) allows parties to express affection and compassion. When violence occurs, the affected parties often feel devalued and dehumanised; hence, showing concern re-members the dis-membered contributing to repairing relations.

One young man Geno asked the officials at the public hearings in Bindura to make provisions for the commission to have offices at the provincial and district level so that more citizens across the country can participate. Currently, the NPRC is housed in Harare and when the public hearings were conducted, they only took place in urban areas, which excluded many of the rural population from participating. Several respondents in the studied communities stated that they were not familiar with the work of the commission and how it would benefit their community. These sentiments highlighted that the NPRC lacks local ownership because it appears to be a project of the political elites and a few urban residents. Seemingly, the commission did not garner confidence from the rural populace which felt excluded, making it difficult to ascertain if the public hearings were inclusive, spread out and deep enough.

Some civil society groups such as the Zimbabwe Civic Education Trust (ZIMCET) tried to bridge the gap by conducting workshops with local communities in the areas covered by their organisation. Through the workshops civil society actors gathered views that they brought forward during the public hearings, rendering them mouthpiece of the citizenry. For instance, Todini a representative from a CSO in Harare shared several challenges he had with the bill key among them was:

I. Lack of security of tenure for appointed commissioners;
II. Presence of the executive in the functions of the commission since the bill required the commissioners to report to the cabinet and not parliament;
III. Permitting the executive to issue ministerial certificate that would prevent a hearing to be heard publicly which denies the public access to information.

These issues raised by Todini were reiterated by several civil society representatives in almost all sessions that I or the research assistants attended in Bindura, Mutare, Marondera, Bulawayo Chinhoyi, Harare and Masvingo. Most attendees of the public hearings from the civil society appreciated the establishment of the commission and the functions it had with regard to addressing past injustices in Zimbabwe. However, they cited several problems that would make the commission less effective in administering the justice that people required. Harumi stated that,

> There is need for the bill to indicate how victims and witnesses will be protected when they come through to the commission. I think torture is a crime against humanity and torture in the bill is not clearly defined, is it from the public officials, the general community, I would want to hear if the commission is going to do something to contribute to the Universal Periodic Reviews of Zimbabwe.

Both Harumi and Todini presented a model for transitional justice that requires the state to align with international standards and regulations, particularly upholding international laws, humanitarian law and human rights law. The South African Truth and Reconciliation Commission (TRC) was even mentioned as an example close to home on which the works of the commission could be modelled with some adjustments. Morreira (2016: 71–72) made similar observations in the deliberations that occurred in workshops she attended involving civil society groups leading up to the creation of the new constitution in 2013. She argued that the rights talk dominated the deliberations and limited the discourse of civil society actors to ideals congruent with the global norms. Even more, the expectation for the commission to contribute to the universal periodic reviews as stated above presented a mandate charged from the global to the local. Hence, the ideas presented on localising transitional justice in Zimbabwe seemed confined to a top-down approach embedded in the liberal peace discourse.

The issue of the global versus local ownership of transitional justice initiatives was expressed by one of the judges in the national courts whom I engaged with during a debriefing session while in the field. Judge Gorimo stated,

> As long as these commissions or tribunals would be funded by Western governments there is no way we can allow them to be established because

> it means they are echelons of the West which are there to fulfil their hidden and foreign agenda, we will never allow that to happen. Us Zimbabweans if we are left to do things on our own, we are good by ourselves and have our own means of dealing with our issues. Remember it is not in our nature to kill each other, *pane nyaya yengozika, upenyu chinhu chakakosha munhu wese anotya ngozi* (there is an issue of avenging spirit [ngozi], life is precious, and everyone is fearful of *ngozi*), I cannot see you ndongokuuraya (and just kill you). Asi mainfluences from outside and societal pressures *ndiwo anoita kuti vanhu vakanganwe nokurasha unhu wedu* (But external influences and societal pressures make people denounce our moral/cultural values).

Even though a legal practitioner, it seemed conflicting that the judge would dismiss support for the commission from Western governments because of hidden agenda. Technocratic justice processes such as the NPRC require huge funds for the initiative to work, and most sponsorship comes from foreign donors which makes the global–local partnership essential for the commission to fulfil its mandate (Zambara 2019). Many similar initiatives on the continent and in the globe were backed by funding from the European Union (EU). For example, the International Criminal Tribunal for Rwanda (ICTR) or the International Criminal Court (ICC) prosecutions, but there remains limited evidence to support successes against the huge costs of these projects (Batamuliza 2009; Clark 2018).

What came out more strongly in my engagements with the judge was a bias towards the stance made by former president Mugabe when Zimbabwe gained independence to 'let by gone be by gones'. Judge Gorimo blamed the violence witnessed in the country since 2000 on external influences and argued that Western governments, mainly members of the EU, have been meddling in internal affairs of Zimbabwe because of the land reclamations done in early 2000s. This view seems to regenerate the idea that the post-2000 era was marred by a justified war, i.e. the Third Chimurenga (Raftopoulos 2009; Ndlovu-Gatsheni 2011). Consequently, parties that were injured or perished were causalities of the war. What I took from this discussion was that the Global North are perceived to be interested in establishing a liberal democratic political order, and whereas state actors in Zimbabwe are keen to 'finish' the project of liberation and emancipation from the Global North. So, these two purposes are working in opposition to one another. The one is trying to establish 'democracy' while the other is trying to preserve its territorial integrity.

An additional complication is that the government has often become an extension of the colonial order it seeks to disregard—they have become an extension of the colonial authorities, colonising their own people (as described by Mamdani 1996 in 'Citizen and subject'). Resultantly, global actors and the state leaders have different expectations; but African governments and their citizens also have different expectations. The government seemingly wants to hold onto power and keep people 'subjected' to them, whereas research participants require social harmony. Therefore, the decolonial project is coming primarily from the people, and not the government per se because justice for the local community is about rebuilding relations between entities in the physical and metaphysical realms, while the government is concerned with reconciliation of political parties.

After attending seven different sessions of the public hearings between 2016 and 2017, I was left wondering whether these meetings had achieved something or were mere window-shopping exercises where various interest groups had showcased ideas of justice informed by norms and values important to them. While transcribing my data, I was intrigued by the remarks of Chimi a middle-aged man who raised this point in Mutare,

> I think this bill is just a brain exercise, government *iri kuda kungonzwawo nyaya* (the government is seeking for relevance). Money is being spent while people pretend to be fixing the country. *Kana tafunga kudya imbwa ngatidyei hono* (If we have considered eating a dog, we must go for a bull [literal meaning]).

The phrase '*kana tafunga kudya imbwa ngatidyei hono*' is a figurative expression that means one should aim on taking full measures or making full commitment when addressing an issue. It is an urge for people to revert on matters by applying themselves fully as this ensures for holistic overhaul to the problem. Chimi's comment suggested a lack of trust in the government and the process being conducted. This lack of trust compromises the legitimacy of state-led processes. I argue that the public hearings of the NPRC bill presented a platform for caucusing on ideas of justice, but many sacrifices were made to develop the NPRC Act. This is common with statist processes because they operate on limited lifespans yet seek to address complex and competing interests, issues, actors and needs (Huyse 1995; Wielenga 2014). In the following section, I look at the outcomes of the commissioned work of the NPRC.

Commissioned Justice

The government of Zimbabwe is currently running the National Peace and Reconciliation Commission (NPRC), which is mandated is to ensure post-conflict justice, healing and reconciliation by (i) encouraging truth-telling, (ii) making of amends (reconciliation), and (iii) provision of justice and rehabilitative treatment (National Peace and Reconciliation Commission 2018a: 12). The commission is also tasked with resolving and mediating disputes as well as setting up institutional frameworks (peace dialogues) and mechanisms for preventing the recurrence of violent conflicts in future. It is backed by the NPRC Act which was signed into law on 5 January 2018 (Muchadehama 2018).

The National Peace and Reconciliation Commission (2018b) strategic plan has described four underlying causes of conflict in Zimbabwe: First is the divisive political culture that polarises communities along political party lines and is permeated through key national institutions, such as the police, judiciary and military, which are supposed to be serving public interests. A militaristic style of governance which was adopted from the colonial era has undermined the capacity of public institutions to deliver services in line with constitutional regulations. This erodes trust of citizens in the state and has created challenges for managing transitions, for example from colonial rule to independence, or elections (Mlambo 2014; Raftopoulos 2009). This suggests that the time frame covered by the commission runs from the colonial to post-colonial era, which accommodates many of the views shared by attendees at the public hearings. However, the lifespan of the commission was not revised making it likely impossible that the initiative will go deep enough.

Second, a culture of violence has implanted fear, mistrust and disunity among citizens. A 53-year-old man from Buhera, Mangwana shared that, "it is difficult to trust anybody because some people are easily persuaded into harming others, especially where political leaders offer them money or food." This lack of trust is increasingly cultivating divisions in a society that already has a history of violence dating to the pre-colonial era. Third, there is a heavy hand or coercive state apparatus devoted to protecting interests of political elites, especially the colonial and ZANU-PF regimes. Fourth, unequal distribution of resources has contributed to deep inequalities within neighbourhoods and across the country and exacerbated socio-economic exclusion and marginalisation. These underlying causes speak to the entrenched culture of violence and political muscle behind, which I believe puts a huge task on the commission to deliver the country from its self-destructive path.

However, the piecemeal workshops and road show campaigns[1] conducted by the commission thus far, render its initiatives momentary events and not deeply invested processes to repair the relational harms that exist within communities. The NPRC remains compromised to drive the justice project in Zimbabwe because of a lack of trust among citizens in the government. More so, it is engulfed with conflicted priorities and unrealistic goals because the government which endorses and finances the initiative is deemed largely responsible for the injustices that the commission is tasked to address (Zambara 2019; Machakanja 2010).

Since 2013, it has taken five years out of the ten-year lifespan of the Peace commission for the government to appoint commissioners and develop an enabling legislature to guide its work. It is less likely that the mandate of the commission will be delivered before its lifespan expires. Even though the NPRC Act was commissioned in January 2018, there is little progress made regarding providing justice and meeting the needs of affected parties (Muchadehama 2018). This delay in establishing supporting structures to enact the work of the commission seemingly suggests that there continues to be a lack of political will and commitment from government pertaining to state-led processes of addressing past injustices (Zambara 2019). With the prevailing financial challenges and shortages of basic commodities, it is unlikely that the government will be able to prioritise funding the commission to fulfil its tasks (Rahim 2019).

Moreover, the government has a history of sweeping the past under the carpet and granting amnesties to perpetrators of violence (Mashingaidze 2005). In response to the injustices of the liberation struggle, the government did not develop any formal policy because the then Prime Minister, Robert Mugabe, resolved to the 'let bygones be bygones', political stance (Eppel and Raftopoulos 2008). Consultations with the affected parties were never undertaken before the government granted forgiveness to perpetrators. Moreover, no room was left for individuals to pursue legal recourse because of the amnesty provision, Clemency Order 1980 (Mashingaidze 2010).

During the Matabeleland massacres (1981–1987), the government commissioned the *Chihambakwe* and *Dumbutshena* Commissions of Inquiry, but their findings remain unknown (CCJP 1997; Mashingaidze 2005). Further amnesties were offered through the Clemency Order of 1988 (CCJP 1997). Similarly, acts of violence that were committed during the fast-track farm invasions and electoral violence since the year 2000 were concealed under amnesty provisions, such as the Clemency Orders of 2000 and 2008 (Solidarity Peace Trust 2008). A complication for the commission is that it is not clear how acts of violence that were pardoned by these amnesties will be revisited.

The actions taken by the Zimbabwean government, for example, political reconciliation over interpersonal reconciliation, and amnesties over redress, give indication to the challenges of state-led processes (Machakanja 2010; Mashingaidze 2010). Often solutions are conceived from the position of balancing power among political antagonists, which leads to the adoption of resolutions that compromise and sacrifice interpersonal relations of parties in affected communities. Statist justice processes are shaped by multiple discourses, driven by global, national or civil society actors, and these have been creating competing priorities that often sacrifice the ordinary citizen.

Justice Gap

The national framework for transitional justice in Zimbabwe (namely the National Peace and Reconciliation Commission Act) seemed fixated on achieving national cohesion and reconciliation. I believe this has constricted the commissioners to a focus on the nation—of which Ndlovu-Gatsheni (2009) has argued Zimbabweans as a nation do not exist—and not the personal/interpersonal relations of people.

What seems urgent in my view is repairing the interpersonal relations of local communities in order to secure a future that is peaceful. The NPRC five-year Strategic Plan (2018–2022) identifies *Ubuntu* as one of the values that inform the work of the commission (others being confidentiality, inclusivity, victim-centredness, transparency) but little is offered to give context to the meanings and outcomes it generates from this principle (National Peace and Reconciliation Commission 2018b: 10). It appears that the term *Ubuntu* which means the same as *Hunhu* is featuring for aesthetic purposes and lacks the moral and spiritual agency it commands from the studied communities (an interpersonal perspective). *Ubuntu* as a fundamental value of the communities studied in this book enshrines justice as *kuenzanisa* (creating a balance or making equal), *kunzwana nhunha* (listening to troubling issues), and *kuringanisa* (making amends or creating a balance) which puts emphasis on repairing interpersonal relations. In rendering *kuenzanisa* or *kunzwana nhunha*, the collaborative efforts of the family/community lighten the burden on the affected parties and often empower the individuals. *Kuenzanisa* retains an equilibrium between the conflicting parties because an injustice destroys the essence of humanity.

Through *kunzwana nhunha*, the community showers the affected party with empathy, which is a crucial component of justice because it gives acknowledgement of the harm done and re-affirms the dignity of the persons involved. The justice pursued seeks to acknowledge the wrongs done and, to make the offender aware of the impact his/her actions have on others. Once an offender has become aware, they take responsibility by reaching out to the affected parties and ask for forgiveness as well as pay any compensation that may be required. This element of creating interpersonal deliberations and offering compensation for the harm incurred fosters social harmony.

Conclusion

Justice is inherently a process of rediscovery, renewal and affirmation of shared values of social groupings. Westendorf (2015) sees justice as a loaded sociopolitical and legal concept that holds varying meanings to different people. Williams (2012: 3) adds that justice during transitions is difficult to administer because real-world conditions require a lot of sacrifices to be made to attain justice, which may include compromising other claims of justice. Therefore, when communities are in transition (i.e. a state of flux), there are multiple contestations that occur around ideas of justice but these should not be silenced by merely adopting universal laws or the views of the powerful.

There is need to engage all other senses that inform the rules by which people govern themselves. I argue that a break away from the violent past can be necessitated by engaging in justice processes that foster spiritual healing to the studied communities because violence has damaged the human spirit and interpersonal relations of entities in the cosmological community. Even though transitional justice may be a contested form of justice, it remains central to peacebuilding and development of states because it enables conflicting parties to imagine the possibility of establishing an alternative political life (Duthie 2008). What remains missing is the understanding of values that should contribute to establishing the new political life and whether the social and spiritual has any place in this process.

I contend that the spiritual and social are essential components of humanity in the studied communities, and life cannot be imagined outside of their interconnectedness as entities in the cosmological community. Violence thus damages not only the physical being or living beings, but also their spirit and that of other spirits embodied in the cosmic community. It breaks the network of relations among cosmic beings and destroys the fruits of their collective harmony. Transitional justice as it pertains to the studied communities is not necessarily a special form of justice but rather an adaptation of varying ideas of justice imbedded in their socio-cultural values to address relational harms and establish a conducive environment that brings harmony to cosmic beings.

Note

1. The NPRC set up the Peace Caravan Campaign in the lead to the 2018 harmonised elections as an avenue to popularise its Peace Pledge and #BuildingBlocks4Peace (National Peace and Reconciliation Commission 2018a). This did not address the political tensions that precipitated the 1 August 2018 shooting by the military in response to protestors following the election on 31 July, or the 14 January 2019 shootings by soldiers during the national protest organised by the ZCTU (Rahim 2019). In both incidents, several civilians were killed, and dozens injured. Most of its work continues to be focusing on reconciling political actors or attending to administrative matters, for example the National Dialogues following the contested 2018 elections and workshops with the parliamentary portfolio committee.

References

Batamuliza, E.A. 2009. The Role of the International Criminal Tribunal for Rwanda in Building Sustainable Peace. Masters Dissertation, Royal Roads University, Canada.

Boraine, A. 2009. South Africa's Truth and Reconciliation Commission from a Global Perspective. In *Peace Versus Justice? The Dilemma of Transitional Justice in Africa*, ed. C.L. Sriram and S. Pillay, 137–152. Scottsville, South Africa: University of KwaZulu-Natal Press.

Bosire, L.K. 2006. Overpromised, Underdelivered: Transitional Justice in Sub-Saharan Africa. *Sur. Revista Internacional de Direitos Humanos* 3 (5): 70–109.

Brounéus, K. 2008. Analyzing Reconciliation: A Structured Method for Measuring National Reconciliation Initiatives. *Peace and Conflict: Journal of Peace Psychology* 14 (3): 291–313.

Catholic Commission for Justice, Peace in Zimbabwe and Legal Resources Foundation (Zimbabwe). 1997. Breaking the Silence, Building True Peace: A Report on the Disturbances in Matabeleland and the Midlands, 1980 to 1988. Catholic Commission for Justice and Peace in Zimbabwe.

Clark, P. 2018. *Distant Justice: The Impact of the International Criminal Court on African Politics*. Cambridge: Cambridge University Press.

Constitution of Zimbabwe. 2013. *Zimbabwe's Constitution of 2013*. Government Publications. Available from https://www.constituteproject.org/constitution/Zimbabwe2013.pdf. Accessed 14 April 2019.

Duthie, R. 2008. Toward a Development-Sensitive Approach to Transitional Justice. *International Journal of Transitional Justice* 2 (3): 292–309.

Eppel, S., and B. Raftopoulos. 2008. *Political Crisis, Mediation and the Prospects for Transitional Justice in Zimbabwe*. Cape Town: IDASA.

Hamber, B., and S. Kibble. 1999. From Truth to Transformation: The Truth and Reconciliation Commission in South Africa. Catholic Institute for International Relations Report. Available from http://csvr.org.za/publications/latest-publications/1714-from-truth-to-transformation-the-truth-and-reconciliation-commission-in-south-africa. Accessed 13 May 2019.

Hayner, P.B. 2010. *Unspeakable Truths: Transitional Justice and the Challenge of Truth Commissions*. New York: Routledge.

Huyse, L. 1995. Justice After Transition: On the Choices Successor Elites Make in Dealing with the Past. *Law & Social Inquiry* 20 (1): 51–78.

Lederach, J.P. 1997. *Building Peace: Sustainable Reconciliation in Divided Societies*. Washington DC: USIP Press.

Machakanja, P. 2010. *National Healing and Reconciliation in Zimbabwe: Challenges and Opportunities*. Cape Town: Institute for Justice and Reconciliation.

Mamdani, M. 1996. *Citizen and Subject: Contemporary Africa and the Legacy of Late Colonialism*. Princeton, NJ: Princeton University Press.

Mashingaidze, T.M. 2005. The 1987 Zimbabwe National Unity Accord and Its Aftermath: A Case of Peace Without Reconciliation. In *From National Liberation to Democratic Renaissance in Southern Africa*, ed. C. Hendricks and L. Lushaba, 82–92. Dakar, Senegal: CODESRIA.

Mashingaidze, T.M. 2010. Zimbabwe's Illusive National Healing and Reconciliation Processes: From Independence to the Inclusive Government 1980–2009. *Conflict Trends* 2010 (1): 19–27.

Mlambo, A.S. 2014. *A History of Zimbabwe*. Cambridge: Cambridge University Press.

Morreira, S. 2016. *Rights After Wrongs: Local Knowledge and Human Rights in Zimbabwe*. Stanford, CA: Stanford University Press.

Muchadehama, A. 2018. *NTJWG Welcomes the NPRC Act*. Available from https://www.newsday.co.zw/2018/01/ntjwg-welcomes-the-nprc-act/. Accessed 12 August 2019.

Murambadoro, R. 2015. 'We Cannot Reconcile Until the Past Has Been Acknowledged': Perspectives of *Gukurahundi* from Matabeleland, Zimbabwe. *African Journal on Conflict Resolution* 47 (1): 31–52.

National Peace and Reconciliation Commission. 2018a. 5-Year Strategic Plan 2018–2022: Transitioning Zimbabwe from a Conflictual Past to a Sustainable, Harmonius & Peaceful Society Through Generations. Available from http://www.nprc.org.zw/sites/default/files/NPRC%202018%20-%202022%20Strategic%20Plan_0.pdf. Accessed 23 June 2019.

National Peace and Reconciliation Commission. 2018b. *National Peace and Reconciliation Commission Regulations SI 90.2018*. Available from http://www.nprc.org.zw/resources/legal-framework/national-peace-and-reconciliation-commission-regulations-si-902018. Accessed 23 June 2019.

National Transitional Justice Working Group. 2016. *NPRC Bill Is Unconstitutional.* Internet. http://www.ntjwg.org/article.php?id=161.

Ndlovu-Gatsheni, S.J. 2009. *Do 'Zimbabweans' Exist? Trajectories of Nationalism, National Identity Formation and Crisis in a Postcolonial State*, vol. 3. Oxford: Peter Lang.

Ndlovu-Gatsheni, S.J. 2011. The Construction and Decline of Chimurenga Monologue in Zimbabwe: A Study in Resilience of Ideology and Limits of Alternatives. Comparative Perspectives from East and Southern Africa paper presented at the 4th European Conference on African Studies (ECAS4), Nordic Africa Institute, June 15–18, Uppsala.

Raftopoulos, B. 2009. The Crisis in Zimbabwe, 1998–2008. In *Becoming Zimbabwe. A History from the Pre-colonial Period to 2008: A History from the Pre-colonial Period to 2008*, ed. B. Raftopoulos and A. Mlambo, 201–232. Avondale, Harare: African Books Collective.

Rahim, Z. 2019. Zimbabwe Protests: Military Deployed After Eight Killed in Fuel Hike Demonstrations. Available from https://www.independent.co.uk/news/world/africa/zimbabwe-protests-today-death-toll-fuel-prices-army-violence-tear-gas-harare-a8729146.html. Accessed 23 November 2019.

Reeler, T. 2016. *Sunday Opinion: The NPRC Bill: Incompetence or Cynicism?* Available from http://www.thestandard.co.zw/2016/01/10/the-nprc-bill-incompetence-or-cynicism/. Accessed 14 September 2019.

Sandoval Villalba, C. 2011. Transitional Justice: Key Concepts, Processes, and Challenges. Institute for Democracy and Conflict Resolution Briefing Paper. Available from http://repository.essex.ac.uk/4482/1/07_11.pdf. Accessed 2 December 2019.

Solidarity Peace Trust 2008. *Punishing Dissent, Silencing Citizens: The Zimbabwe Elections 2008.* Available from http://www.solidaritypeacetrust.

org/download/report-files/punish_and_silence.pdf. Accessed 4 September 2019.

Villa-Vicencio, C. 2007. Transitional Justice, Restoration, and Prosecution. In *Handbook of Restorative Justice: A Global Perspective*, ed. D. Sullivan and L. Tifft, 387–400. London: Routledge.

Westendorf, J.K. 2015. *Why Peace Processes Fail: Negotiating Insecurity After Civil War*. Boulder: Lynne Rienner Publishers.

Wielenga, C. 2014. Reconciliation from the Top Down? Government Institutions in South Africa, Rwanda and Burundi. *Strategic Review for Southern Africa* 36 (1): 25–46.

Wielenga, C., Z. Matsimbe, and R. Murambadoro. 2015. The Liberal Peacebuilding Framework, Electoral Democracy and Reconciliation: The Cases of Mozambique and Zimbabwe. In *Election Processes Management and Election-Based Violence in Eastern and Southern Africa*, ed. P.B. Mihyo. OSSREA: Ethiopia.

Williams, M. 2012. *Transitional Justice: NOMOS LI.* NYU Press. *Project MUSE*. Available from muse.jhu.edu/book/20735. Accessed 24 October 2019.

Zambara, W. 2019. *Prospects for Social Cohesion, Healing and Reconciliation in Zimbabwe: Putting the NPRC to Task.* Institute for Justice and Reconciliation. Available from https://www.ijr.org.za/2019/09/16/the-prospects-for-social-cohesion-healing-and-reconciliation-in-zimbabwe-putting-the-nprc-to-task/. Accessed 24 October 2019.

Zimbabwe Human Rights NGO Forum. 2016. *NPRC Bill Is Unconstitutional.* Available from http://www.hrforumzim.org/news/nprc-bill-is-unconstitutional/. Accessed 12 November 2019.

6

Conclusion: Transitional Justice in Zimbabwe—Myth or Reality?

Abstract Challenges often occur in administering transitional justice in post-colonial states in Africa and Zimbabwe because of competing goals between state-centric and human-centred approaches. Customary justice process though plausible for communities studied in this book, they are often side-lined on the assumption that they are archaic and incompatible with human rights. What was clear in my interactions with research participants from Buhera, Mudzi and Uzumba is the idea harms pollute the cosmological community and require a concomitant tradition-based remedy. The functional value of customary justice processes covered in this book is not to only uphold the rights of an afflicted individual but to restore the psychosocial well-being of individuals in relation to their community through a holistic approach that transforms effects of violence on cosmic beings.

Keywords Transitional justice · Living customary law · Customary justice · Human relations · Interpersonal · Socio-cultural values

R. Murambadoro, *Transitional Justice in Africa*, Development, Justice and Citizenship, https://doi.org/10.1007/978-3-030-48092-9_6

Introduction

The entry point of this book was to offer context-based understandings of violence, peace and justice as well as processes that occur to violence-stricken communities in Zimbabwe to facilitate rebuilding social harmony. State-sanctioned violence experienced by research participants in this study metamorphosised into a psychosocial state that transformed interpersonal relations of entities in their communities. It disrupted human relations of persons who share the same space with the individual directly affected by violence and those who witnessed it and the afterlife. African beings in this study do not exist in isolation; they belong to social groupings to which they have duties and responsibilities. They are social actors who when affected by violence, their experiences take a hold on their community, and continue to be passed on through generations, each creating its own wounds. Justice conceived in this book is therefore, more than the mere resolution of political disputes that has occurred at the national level. It attends to the well-being of the community amending the web of interconnected beings which make up the African community. In this chapter, I offer a conclusion of the book by attending to the question: Is transitional justice a myth or reality for communities in Zimbabwe affected by violence?

A Recap of the Book

Transitional justice is a concept within the peacebuilding discourse that has travelled across continents, it has been transposed and translated to suit varying contexts where communities are seeking to address their painful pasts. A grappling point for many practitioners and scholars of transitional justice has been to ascertain what transitional justice means to different actors and contexts, as well as at different moments or levels. The contestations around which approach to take in administering justice at the national level is fuelled by the competing goals that the concept transitional justice is embedded with.

For Roht-Arriaza (2006: 2), transitional justice is a 'set of practices, mechanisms and concerns that arise following a period of conflict, civil strife or repression, and that are aimed at dealing with past violations of human rights and humanitarian law'. Branch (2014: 610) defines transitional justice as a discourse, set of practices and institutions that facilitate political remedy for past injustices through present justice. Arthur (2009: 324) describes transitional justice as a 'field' comprised of 'an international web of individuals and institutions, whose internal coherence is held together by common concepts, practical aims and distinctive claims for legitimacy' that are demonstrated in attempts to address violations associated with political change. More so, Bell (2009: 6) proposes that transitional justice is a 'label or cloak that aims to rationalize a set of diverse bargains in relation to the past, as an integrated endeavour, to obscure the quite different normative, moral and political implications of the bargains'. All these definitions provide an indication of competing understandings around what transitional justice entails and the processes for administering it.

Most participants in this study were unable to provide the local meaning of the concept of transitional justice. They offered definitions for the term justice, using the words *kuenzanisa* (creating a balance or making equal), *kunzwana nhunha* (listening to troubling issues) and *kuringanisa* (making amends or creating a balance). Justice involves *kuraira* (giving counsel), *kuranga* (instilling discipline), *kudzoredzanisa* (reconciling) and *kuripira* (reparations) and is understood as a doing word that commands actions, affirmations and interactions to facilitate a process of reflection, engagement and healing to the damaged cosmos. The focus of this book has been on the effect of politically motivated violence on human relations of local communities. What can be observed is that political contestations, especially in the post-2000 period involving the ZANU-PF and MDC parties, have infiltrated the family structure at the community level and destroyed human and social relations of people in Buhera, Mudzi and Uzumba. It is increasingly harder for members of the same family who belong to different political organisations to trust each other and uphold the socio-cultural values of their community.

These interpersonal rifts breed enmity, resentment and intolerance that makes some to view others as sell-outs that need to be dealt with. The binaries of insider versus outsider or sell-out versus patriot have become a key feature in the political engagements occurring at national level but filtering into local communities. A danger with this divisionism at the community level is that rural areas of Zimbabwe, such as Buhera, Mudzi and Uzumba, are made of family groupings that have settled along their clan lines. For example, Buhera has six clan groupings namely *Museyamwa*, *Sinyoro*, *Dziva*, *Murozvi*, *Nyathi* and *Moyo*. Clan names provide a socio-cultural identity to members of the family. There are strong socio-cultural ties among clan members and a sense of collective acceptable conduct because people are connected through their ancestral lineage, inter-clan marriages, common language and land. *Imba* (the home) is therefore, an important feature in the livelihoods of research participants because they live communally and are related through their clan lines. Actions of persons in this living arrangement are sanctioned by their constituent social grouping because of the living customary laws they subscribe to denoted in *Hunhu* and *tsika nemagariro*.

Political contestations are eroding the socio-cultural values that bind local communities to live in harmony. Their co-values require people to *kugara nevamwe zvakanaka* (live in harmony), *kuzvininipisa* (being humble), *kudyidzana* (friendship or fellowship), *kuzvibata* (self-discipline), *rukudzo* (respect), *kushanda nesimba* (industrious) and *kudzoreka* (teachable spirit), among others. Hence acts of violence which they referred to as *mhirizhonga* (violence, instability or disorder), *bopoto* (quarrelling), *kurwisana* (fighting), *makakatanwa* (tensions), *bvongamupopoto* (disruptive behaviour), *bvonga bvonga* (chaos), *nyonganiso* (chaos or disruptions) and z*howe zhowe* (chaos) capture the harms that occur to relations of the people at interpersonal level. Violence does not only affect an individual but destroys the network of relations that exist among people because *munhu wese ihama* (everyone is family).

Hunhu is thus a normative framework that locates *vanhu vatema* (African beings) covered in this study as interdependent entities who strive to bring the best in society by respecting and valuing the essence of life that all beings possess. *Unhu* as an African embodiment is observed through traits that one possesses and from these, they attract fortune.

The Shona proverb *chisi hachieri musi wacharimwa* (which means a wrong action may not reap immediate remedial action) captures the functional value of *hunhuism* in guiding actions of the studied communities regarding sanctioning human relations. Positive and negative traits attract omen which can make one prosper in life (i.e. good fortune) or encounter misfortunes (possessed by a bad omen). When violence occurs, it is a display of bad traits which attract bad omen on the individual and community. Hence it is crucial among the local communities to foster virtuous qualities because they contribute to their well-being physically and metaphysically.

Transitional justice within the context of communities covered in this book refers to an adaptation of varying ideas of justice imbedded in their socio-cultural values to address relational harms and establish a conducive environment that brings harmony to cosmic beings. A disconnect between international legal norms and local priorities and practices of justice is that the living customary law they uphold is not accusatory, rather it is inquisitorial. When families perform a *dare* to resolve a dispute, all members are involved and contribute towards repairing relations of the family. What can be observed as an underlying thread in the studied communities is the understanding that human values are built on the reciprocal recognition of humanity and that rights are correlative with duties. It is therefore problematic to divest people from their culture, history and being just to make way for the modelling of the society in the Western perspective of human rights (Cobbah 1987). More so, it is unimaginable that the *vanhu vatema* (African beings) covered in this book would be able to respond to their natural passions and wishes outside the realm of their social world (which is made up of the physical and metaphysical realms). Their rights and obligations knit together the community through interdependent relations that include the individual, the extended family and the whole society.

Concluding Thoughts

When we consider Africanising transitional justice to match the customs and traditions of the concerned parties, the tendency is to equate African justice systems to customary law. What is considered as customary law in Zimbabwe is usually the Customary law and Local Courts Act (Chapter 7: 5), which was developed during the colonial era. Himonga et al. (2014) consider these provisions to be official customary law, and that it is different from the living customary law exercised in the everyday by African communities. On the contrary, the living customary law emanates from the living norms that regulate the everyday of people's lives and forged through constant interactions of the people (Diala 2017). These living customary laws are not static rather generated through interactions of people within a context over time.

Another push back on customary justice processes within the peacebuilding discourse has been the view that customary practices apply mostly to people living in the rural areas and not the city. Those in the city are considered to be cosmopolitan and more attuned to state laws. This view fails to observe that Africans no longer live in towns and villages with different sets of insulated rules, rather their lives are guided by plural norms which traverse each other (Chirayath et al. 2005). Many people in Zimbabwe live their lives in multiple interfaces that involve the urban and rural, the physical and metaphysical, as well as the global, national or local. It is misguiding therefore, to separate and insulate the customary sphere, as if it is a component that is devoid of other interfaces that make up realities of *vanhu vatema* (African beings).

Attention should be placed on understanding the multiple interfaces that inform the relations, behaviours and actions of a social grouping within its context. For instance, when African Zimbabweans meet for the first time whether in the urban or rural space, their first interactions tend to revolve around getting acquainted with each other. A common question that is asked is *unobvepi?* (where do you come from?), to which one can respond, '*ndinobva kwa*Nerutanga' (I come from Nerutanga), '*asi ndine imba ku*Harare so *ndikwo kwandinogara nekushanda*' (but I have a house in Harare where I stay and work). The rural space represents an interface of origin which informs one's identity within the social grouping because it is through this origin that one can trace their lineage and networks of relations that link them to others in their surroundings. In many cases, the urban space (such as Harare mentioned above) provides temporary residency and is a temporal spatiality, hence when one dies in the city, they are often taken back to their rural home for burial, which is part of African customs.

A question that often comes to mind is: Can one return to an African justice system informed by living customary laws, and forego human rights? Is it possible for human rights and living customary laws to co-exist? A Zimbabwean human rights lawyer Beatrice Mtetwa stated in an interview with Trevor Ncube that human rights are not Eurocentric or foreign to Zimbabwe; they are universal and should be enjoyed by everyone (Mtetwa 2019). In the Zimbabwean context, the human rights discourse has enabled several reforms to occur within the legal framework at both the national and local level (for instance, the changes to the ngozi practice mentioned in Chapter 4 of this book) and to some extent changes have been effected in the country's political landscape. For example, Andrew Meldrum was the first journalist to be prosecuted by the state using the draconian law, the Access to Information and Protection of Privacy Act (AIPPA) of 2002. In the view of Mtetwa who was representing Meldrum in 2002, the magistrate who heard the case ruled in their favour, taking recognition of the flaws in the actions of the state. But she went on to mention that Meldrum was acquitted at the magistrate's court, and if the case had gone to the Supreme Court the outcome could have been unfavourable.

The interviewee asked Mtetwa, the implications of the different outcomes on the state of the national judicial system in Zimbabwe? She explained that when the complainant is the state and the defendant is a citizen, the case succeeds to court hearings and in many instances the defendant is acquitted. However, when the complainant is the citizen and the defendant is the state, such matters often fall out without being resolved. This scenario gives a compromised relationship between the state and the citizens. The judiciary is captured, especially the higher courts (Constitutional Court, Supreme Court, High Court) responsible for administering justice and upholding human rights. This infestation of the judiciary system has been carried over from the Mugabe regime (which is responsible for the acts of violence covered in this book), to Mnangagwa's regime, which is also facing its own cases of violent action against civilians (Rahim 2019).

This raises a further question: Is the NPRC (which is a state-led process) suitable to deliver justice to the people of Zimbabwe who have been affected by the varying episodes of state-sanctioned violence? Basing on the insights about the judiciary systems offered by Mtetwa stated above and experiences of research participants in the study, it is unlikely that justice will be attained through static transitional mechanisms. What was clear in my interactions with research participants from Buhera, Mudzi and Uzumba is the idea that bad actions pollute the cosmological community and require a concomitant cleansing ritual, ceremony and compensation, for example, *magadziro*, *chenura*, *kubvunzira* and *kuripira ngozi*. Failure to repair human relations harbours toxic traits for example *shanje* (jealous), *kusanzwirana* (tensions) which can beget further harms on the community. *Kuripisana* (reparations) is a form of caution to the wrongdoers but also restorative in that the receiving party gets tangible possessions they can use for their upkeep.

The studied communities believe that y*adeuka yadeuka* (when a wrong is done it cannot be reversed) so there is no remedy that equates to the harm, rather a reparation is symbolic and meant to provide recognition of the harm incurred. People work on *kuwonesana* (bringing understanding) and openness because they help to restore social harmony. This does not suggest that people do not have disputes, grudges or divisions but rather their differences and misgivings should not be harboured hence the constant engagement and need for upholding shared virtues. From a scholarly and practical point, I have had to grapple with the question: How can one develop these perspectives into a transitional justice framework that fits the African setting and inform the global peace project?

After effects of violence in the studied communities are perpetual fear and disruption of harmony. The more people talk about it the more it invites discussion and redress. The power of the spoken word when people speak ugly about one's actions is that it attracts bad omen because *pasi panonzwa* (the ancestors hear). When people speak ugly about one's actions, it is considered *kugunun'una* or *kunyunyuta*, which are expressions of displeasure that evoke bad omen. The functional value of these expressions lies in the belief that all actions good and ugly, attract a commensurate reaction or response. The idea is therefore not to only uphold the rights of an afflicted individual but to restore their psychosocial well-being through a holistic approach that transforms effects of violence on cosmic beings.

This book offers an understanding of justice that is embedded in socio-cultural values of the research participants. Justice begins with the human experience; it should be grounded in current practices of enforcing mutual responsibilities embedded in the contexts in which violence occurred. Understanding the interconnectedness of human relations to experiences of violence creates room to acknowledge who people are as individuals and within their family and community. This aids to understand the disruptions that occur to human relations and the community they exist in when violence occurs, as well as processes required to repair relationships.

For Zimbabwe to recover from the current sociopolitical and economic problems, it is facing there is a need therefore, to establish non-party consensual democracy (Wiredu 1995) built on the socio-cultural values embedded in the philosophy of *Hunhu*. There is need to instil positive virtues that such as *kudyidzana* (friendship or fellowship), *kuzvibata* (self-discipline), *rukudzo* (respect), *kudzoreka* (teachable spirit) within the community and among people of different political affiliations. African values instil the understanding that all actions have a commensurate reaction, whether good or bad. The reactions will not only affect an individual but the whole community because *munhu wese ihama*. Understanding that everyone is a part of a bigger community gives essence and new meaning to the humanity of individuals within conflict riddled communities. This enables them to see the essence of life outside of their political associations but in harmony with others and intertwined to the physical and metaphysical. Justice during transitions from an African perspective brings a renewal of life and restores virtues that enable communities to uphold human relations because they give essence to humanity.

References

Arthur, P. 2009. How ‘Transitions’ Reshaped Human Rights: A Conceptual History of Transitional Justice. *Human Rights Quarterly* 31 (2): 321–367.

Bell, C. 2009. Transitional Justice, Interdisciplinarity and the State of the ‘Field’ or ‘Non-field’. *International Journal of Transitional Justice* 3 (1): 5–27.

Branch, A. 2014. The Violence of Peace: Ethnojustice in Northern Uganda. *Development and Change* 45 (3): 608–630.

Chirayath, L., C. Sage, and M. Woolcock. 2005. Customary Law and Policy Reform: Engaging with the Plurality of Justice Systems. World Development Report Background Papers. Available from https://openknowledge.worldbank.org/handle/10986/9075. Accessed 26 September 2019.

Cobbah, J.A. 1987. African Values and the Human Rights Debate: An African Perspective. *Human Rights Quarterly* 9 (3): 309–331.

Diala, A.C. 2017. The Concept of Living Customary Law: A Critique. *The Journal of Legal Pluralism and Unofficial Law* 49 (2): 143–165.

Himonga, C., T. Nhlapo, I.P. Maithufi, M.S. Weeks, L. Mofokeng, and D. Ndima. 2014. *African Customary Law in South Africa: Post-Apartheid and Living Law Perspectives*. Cape Town: Oxford University Press Southern Africa.

Mtetwa, B. 2019. Beatrice Mtetwa in Conversation with Trevor (Part 1). Available from https://www.youtube.com/watch?v=EiICfo86lIo. Accessed 1 November 2019.

Rahim, Z. 2019. *Zimbabwe Protests: Military Deployed After Eight Killed in Fuel Hike Demonstrations*. Available from https://www.independent.co.uk/news/world/africa/zimbabwe-protests-today-death-toll-fuel-prices-army-violence-tear-gas-harare-a8729146.html. Accessed 23 November 2019.

Roht-Arriaza, N. 2006. *The Pinochet Effect: Transnational Justice in the Age of Human Rights*. Philadelphia: University of Pennsylvania Press.

Wiredu, K. 1995. Democracy and Consensus in African Traditional Politics: A Plea for a Non-party Polity. *The Centennial Review* 39 (1): 53–64.

Index

R. Murambadoro, *Transitional Justice in Africa*, Development, Justice and Citizenship, https://doi.org/10.1007/978-3-030-48092-9

CPI Antony Rowe
Eastbourne, UK
July 07, 2020